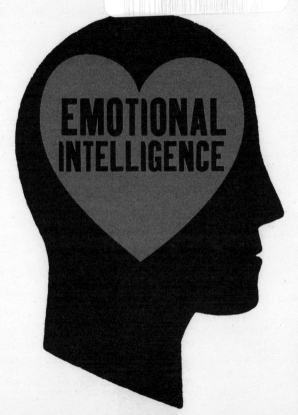

EMOTIONAL INTELLIGENCE

DR DAVID WALTON

A PRACTICAL GUIDE

Published in the UK
in 2012 by Icon Books Ltd,
Omnibus Business Centre,
39–41 North Road,
London N7 9DP
email: info@iconbooks.com
www.iconbooks.com

Sold in the UK, Europe and Asia
by Faber & Faber Ltd,
Bloomsbury House,
74–77 Great Russell Street,
London WC1B 3DA
or their agents

Distributed in South Africa
by Jonathan Ball,
Office B4, The District,
41 Sir Lowry Road,
Woodstock 7925

Distributed in Australia and
New Zealand
by Allen & Unwin Pty Ltd,
PO Box 8500,
83 Alexander Street,
Crows Nest,
NSW 2065

Distributed in Canada
by Publishers Group Canada,
76 Stafford Street, Unit 300
Toronto,
Ontario M6J 2S1

Distributed in the USA
by Publishers Group West,
1700 Fourth Street,
Berkeley, CA 94710

ISBN: 978-184831-422-1

Typeset in Avenir by Marie Doherty

Printed and bound in the UK by Clays Ltd, St Ives plc

About the author

David Walton trained initially as a clinical psychologist in the UK's National Health Service, then as an occupational psychologist in government and public service. He worked in the UK and North America for a leading behavioural science consultancy and was subsequently principal psychologist with the United Nations Research Institute for Social Development.

In a varied career, David has advised the European Commission on people and organizational development projects and individuals and organizations in the private and public sectors on management and staff development. He holds visiting fellowships at two UK universities and is a national mentor for two very large social care charities. David also devises community education programmes helping people to understand more about mental health, depression, cognitive therapy and child and adolescent development.

Author's note

It is important to note that there are many ideas and research findings that are frequently cited in relation to emotional intelligence. Where we know the origin we have been sure to reference it. Our apologies to the originators of any material who have been inadvertently overlooked.

Contents

Introduction

What is emotional intelligence all about?

Take a look at the following people. Do they remind you of anyone you know?

Anthony is trying to decide whether to cash in a savings bond to buy a classic car he wants. The trouble is, if he keeps the bond for another six months, it will mature and he will get an extra £5,000. But the car will have gone and it's special. He wants it badly. He's already got three other cars but he's not good on delayed gratification. Things would be easier if he had regular work.

Sue doesn't get on with her chief executive despite doing a really good job. He's incredibly dismissive, doesn't respond to her reports on things which need looking at or approaching differently – and he never looks her in the eye. Her colleagues see her as a role model for good practice. She wants a good career but isn't sure about the next step.

Peta hasn't met her sales targets again. Her customers just like to talk about their problems. She doesn't have anything in common with those sorts of people and would rather just get on with the job.

Peter gets very frustrated at home. His wife has changed. Nothing seems to satisfy her anymore and he has only the vaguest notion why. She seems frustrated or depressed all the time, in equal measure. She thinks he's

1

always at fault so he gets angry, slamming doors and walking away.

Like many people, these individuals are all struggling with situations and difficulties which are troubling to different degrees. At first sight, it seems as though logic, rational decision-making and perhaps good common sense are the answer – in theory, that is. But these examples come from the real world. Anthony, Sue and the others are real people. And that means they aren't always logical. They don't always use rational decision-making, or common sense, for that matter.

Instincts, feelings and personal values take over and become a major part of the dilemmas facing our four people. Conflict between our thinking and our feelings makes things complicated. Gut instincts or intuition rely a great deal on emotion and feelings. The real world is a place where both feelings and instincts are major influences on our behaviour.

Anthony for example is having difficulty resisting temptation. He could wait for a lot more money – his logic might tell him – but the demands made by his emotions are in conflict with this. What actually happened was that, as usual, he gave way to his emotions and cashed in his savings bond. A year later he was in dire financial circumstances – not just because of the car, but because the struggle between logic and emotion was always won in the same way. His feelings seem to take over his thinking: he makes a great case to himself for anything he wants.

Sue is trying to balance her own anxieties with the way her organization is changing and the effect of this change on the views and approaches of her colleagues. Her need for recognition is very high. She works with people who don't express themselves emotionally nor understand the importance of this for motivating staff. A year on, she has left her job. The organization has lost a real asset.

Peta hoped that her sales performance could be good enough without engaging too closely with her customers. She is uncomfortable getting too close to people. She finds small talk difficult and has always coped by concentrating on things she is interested in. Her product knowledge is good but it doesn't seem to affect her performance. She is now working in a back-office role, at a lower salary.

Peter is struggling to find ways of bringing his relationship under control. He and his wife are strong characters but he has never felt able to confront problems between them. He thinks it is better to walk away when he is angry because he has difficulty controlling strong emotions. His wife thinks he has become cold and is now wondering whether her life could be more fulfilling.

In each of the situations described above, the people involved will benefit from improving their emotional intelligence (EI). Their doing so will also make life easier for those who have to interact with them. EI is a valuable set of ideas you can use in the workplace and in the home; as a parent, teacher or manager.

It's about being aware of feelings in yourself and in others, understanding them and managing their impact. It's about being in control, interpreting body language, coping with negativity, working with others and building psychological well-being.

So what is this book *actually* about?

Emotional intelligence is an assortment of mental abilities and skills that can help you to successfully manage both yourself and the demands of working with others.

Developing your own EI enables you to:
- Know yourself reasonably well
- Control your own emotions
- Show empathy with the feelings of others
- Use social skills in an effective as well as simply pleasant way.

This involves:
- **Mindfulness:** being aware – understanding yourself and others
- **Being in control** of your own thoughts, emotions and needs
- **Being positive and self-motivated** particularly in the face of setbacks

- **Using empathy:** being able to put yourself in others' shoes
- **Communicating effectively** to build productive and positive relationships
- **Using emotional reasoning:** being able to use emotions to enhance rather than restrict your thinking.

Hundreds of books have been written about emotional intelligence. It has been defined in many ways, usually depending on the interests or academic discipline of the person writing about it. As the idea has been explored and different models developed, it has become one of the most talked-about ideas in popular psychology, industrial training, in management, education and social care. Emotional intelligence has been touted as an explanation of what your brain does, a means to achieve your goals, a basis for improving your family life and relationships, improving your job prospects and being more successful at work. Outcomes at one level are managing stress better, coping with depression and overcoming anxiety. For others it is a way to become a better negotiator, getting better deals or increased sales. I have even seen a cookery programme on TV which suggested that emotional intelligence is the key to good dinner parties!

If all of this is true, EI must be one of the most significant areas explored in psychology over the last 50 years. At the very least, it can be a real stimulus for exploring psychology

– and in the process helping to make some of its powerful ideas relevant and accessible to living and working in today's world.

At its most basic, emotional intelligence is the ability to manage the impact of emotions on our relationships with others. It involves recognizing accurately how you and others feel at any particular time and the way emotions are affecting the situation. It involves keeping feelings sufficiently in control so that we can act effectively. And in no small part it involves using good interpersonal skills to create positive relationships with both individuals and groups. Our ability to express the emotions we feel in a constructive way is the cornerstone of staying in control.

EI is based on an important feature of relationships: 'behaviour breeds behaviour'. Our own approach may be the cause of others' reactions. Emotional intelligence requires us to be mindful of the effect we have.

A general consensus amongst the more recent models of EI is that, whether in work or personal relationships, emotional intelligence can be learned. Teaching ourselves to be mindful about the way both we and others feel can help us work towards mutually rewarding relationships. And in times of economic difficulty, the difference between productive and unproductive relationships can make the difference between surviving or not.

So the goal of this book is simple. It's to provide you with a practical understanding of how the idea of emotional intelligence emerged, what people say it is, why it is important for you, and some tools to help you develop your own EI.

Sound useful? Good. But emotional intelligence is not really new, and the skills and abilities involved have not always been a positive thing. As long ago as the 16th century, Niccolo Machiavelli was writing about 'accounting of feelings and needs' as an important set of tools in his attempts to seek influence with the Pope to become more powerful himself. Manipulation, politics and deceit may all owe much to the emotional intelligence of those practising the dark arts for their own advancement. And if you believe the press about the devious machinations of our current politicians, that view may be more true today than ever before.

On the one hand, there are times when being clear, firm or even tough with others is a necessary part of being effective. But on the other, as we gain more experience in both personal and working relationships, it is clear that being forceful isn't right for all situations. Social skills like understanding others' needs, generating shared goals, knowing their motivation and aspirations, negotiating, providing support, and diplomacy may be needed. Conflict resolution, with restraint and self-control at times, are important tools for getting on with others.

I recently heard a leading academic who is responsible for running a major university say, 'Everything would be fine if it weren't for the students and the staff! Sometimes I don't know which is which.' Most of us already know that

7

whilst intellectual skills are important, you can't get through life without having to deal with other people. Maybe that academic needs to use her emotional intelligence every bit as much as her intellectual skills to create the impact she would like.

Some of the more specific benefits of developing EI include the ability to:

- Overcome difficult situations
- Express yourself clearly but warmly
- Build better relationships
- Keep your emotions under control
- Communicate mutual respect
- Avoid skewed thinking
- Say the appropriate thing at the right time
- Value and obtain commitment from others
- Become resilient in difficult times
- Have clear values and share them with others
- Increase your own well-being.

So why do people appear to have very different levels of emotional intelligence? There is a great debate about EI as to whether it comes from nature or nurture. Is EI is a set of innate skills like numeracy and logic? (Perhaps they simply haven't developed yet in some people.) Or is it something which is akin to personality – perhaps traits or characteristics which are genetic or acquired over time? Perhaps some people are simply 'people people'. Leaving the academic debates to one side, it is clear that there are certain skills and abilities which have been found to be of real and practical value in the most surprising situations.

CASE STUDY

Can emotional intelligence save your life?
James Dozier, a brigadier general in the US Army was kidnapped in 1981 while on duty in Italy. His captors were the notorious Red Brigade terrorists. Writing about his experiences, Dozier noted the effect of media coverage on the kidnap team: 'they were bouncing off the walls with anxiety and pressure and were becoming explosively dangerous. A wrong look could have got me killed.' It was an increasingly risk-laden situation. Dozier's training had included some aspects of emotional management and he decided to try to minimize the risks by using what we might now call emotional intelligence. He set out to manage his own feelings of anxiety and to see what effect it could have on the Red Brigade terrorists. Although bound, he tried to make himself communicate as calmly as possible, showing concern for his captors and modelling the behaviours he thought were needed to reduce the terrorists' own anxiety. As he hoped, their tension and tendency towards spontaneous reactions reduced as the captors began to respond to his confident, slow and reflective manner.

After his release, Dozier explained that his experience led him to believe that understanding the emotional

9

dynamics at work in the situation, and his ability to manage his own emotions and behaviour, actually saved his life.

How to use this book

Throughout the book there are a number of activities for you to try, notes for you to read and things for you to remember.

Within this introduction, we will explore the foundations on which emotional intelligence is based, including what we know about intelligence itself, what causes the emotions which drive us, and how our brain's control system is 'hard-wired' to them. We will also look at the opposite of EI: keeping a 'stiff upper lip', and why being tough and hard has been prized for so long.

In Part I, 'The Emotional Intelligence Framework', we will explore the practical skills and knowledge which emotional intelligence promotes.

Part II of the book, 'Emotional Intelligence in Practice', deals with some specific uses of emotional intelligence. We will look at what occupational psychology tells us about the workplace – the area where EI exploded into life 20 years ago. We will also explore its use in education, parenting and healthcare, and look at how it can be used for simply making your life better.

REMEMBER THIS!!! If you use any of the questionnaires in this book, remember that they are guides, not fully validated psychometric tests. They have been tested in various companies and occupational groups, in adult education and with different ethnic groups. They seem to be useful – but see what you think!

Can you teach an old dog new tricks?

If you are prepared to do some thinking, to reflect on ideas from other people's experience and to both challenge and discipline yourself to improve, this book should help you understand EI. But if you are the sort of person who believes that changing your personality or behaviour is not possible – that 'you can't teach an old dog new tricks' – you need to know something before you read on.

You possess one of nature's great miracles – your AMAZING BRAIN! We will look at the way it works and some of its physical structures later. But from an old dog's point of view, you need to know *before you start* that, if you want to, you *can* change yourself and your approach. It's something your brain can do for you and involves something called 'plasticity'.

Whatever age you are now, your life so far has been spent building up behavioural templates, which are stored in your brain and used for reacting automatically to situations. These are pathways between brain cells that get more fixed as feelings and thought patterns are repeated.

They are physical things – proteins attached to your DNA and neural connections controlling your behaviours. They are central. They define you.

You are not starting from scratch. If nothing else, your experience of living and working with others will have already have given you opportunities to develop your emotional intelligence. As a teenager, your brain rapidly developed pathways to deal with particular situations in certain ways. You may have become good at evaluating things, calculating risks or working out solutions. You may or may not have developed pathways which help you deal with other people and emotional situations. You can use this book to assess how well you have done so far.

One of the key discoveries in neuroscience over the last fifteen years has been that we are able to make our brains actually grow. It happens through a process called neurogenesis in which brain cells or neurons grow and proliferate, migrating to where they may be needed. Pathways or routes of interconnecting neurons develop through daily use – in the same way that a path down a bank might be developed when it is used daily by an animal going about its business.

Every time new knowledge is acquired, the connections communicate differently and, through repetition, become faster, more efficient and instinctive. The ability of our brains to develop in this way is described as 'synaptic plasticity'. So the good news is that we do change. Unlearning old behaviours and forming new emotional intelligence templates happen all the time – if you have the motivation and the space for thinking it out.

 The bottom line is that we all have the capacity to develop new thinking and behaviour if we are sufficiently motivated. So not only can you learn about EI, you can learn to put it into practice.

In the remainder of this introduction we will go on to discuss the foundations and context for EI. For starters, though, try the following questionnaire to start forming an idea of your own levels of EI.

 Measuring emotional intelligence
Here is a quiz, which is an example of the many tests that are now available. The results you get from this quiz are NOT a comprehensive picture of your EI but will provide some useful insights into both the skills it involves and how tests measure them.

There are ten situations. For each, read the four actions and choose which of them is closest to the way you would

13

be likely to behave if you were in a similar situation. Choose your *actual behaviour* rather than what you think you *should* do. Make a note of your choice and go through the scoring page carefully. In addition to getting a 'quick and dirty' measure of your own EI, the answers will give you a sense of the key skill sets involved.

1. You are on an aeroplane that suddenly hits extremely bad turbulence and begins rocking from side to side. What do you do?

A. Continue to read your book or magazine, or watch the movie, trying to pay little attention to the turbulence.

B. Become vigilant for an emergency, carefully monitoring the cabin staff and reading the emergency instructions card.

C. A little of both A and B.

D. Not sure – you probably never noticed.

2. You are in a meeting when a colleague takes credit for work that you have done. What do you do?

A. Immediately and publicly confront the colleague over the ownership of your work.

B. After the meeting, take the colleague aside and tell her that you would appreciate in the future that she credits you when speaking about your work.

C. Nothing, it's not a good idea to embarrass colleagues in public.

D. After the colleague speaks, publicly thank her for referencing your work and give the group more specific detail about what you were trying to accomplish.

3. You are a customer service representative and are speaking to an extremely angry client on the phone. What do you do?

A. Hang up. You aren't paid to take abuse from anyone.

B. Listen to the client and rephrase what you gather he is feeling.

C. Explain to the client that he is being unfair, that you are only trying to do your job, and you would appreciate it if he wouldn't get in the way of this.

D. Tell the client you understand how frustrating this must be for him, and offer a specific thing you can do to help him get his problem resolved.

4. You are a college student who had hoped to get an A in an exam that was important for your future career aspirations. You have just found out you achieved a C–. What do you do?

A. Sketch out a specific plan for ways to improve your mark and resolve to follow it through.

B. Decide you do not have what it takes to make it in that career.

C. Tell yourself it really doesn't matter how well you do in the course; concentrate instead on other classes where your marks are higher.

D. Go and discuss your results with your tutor and try to talk her into giving you a better mark.

5. *You are a manager in an organization that is trying to encourage respect for racial and ethnic diversity. You overhear someone telling a racist joke. What do you do?*

A. Ignore it – the best way to deal with these things is not to react.

B. Call the person into your office and explain that their behaviour is inappropriate and is grounds for disciplinary action if repeated.

C. Speak up on the spot, saying that such jokes are inappropriate and will not be tolerated in your organization.

D. Suggest to the person telling the joke that he attend a diversity training course.

6. *You are an insurance salesman calling on prospective clients. You have had no success with your last fifteen clients. What do you do?*

A. Call it a day and go home early to miss rush-hour traffic.

B. Try something new in the next call, and keep plugging away.

C. List your strengths and weaknesses to identify what may be undermining your ability to sell.

D. Sharpen up your resumé.

7. You are trying to calm down a colleague who has worked herself into a fury because the driver of another car has swerved dangerously close to her car. What do you do?

A. Tell her to forget about it – she's OK now and it is no big deal.

B. Put on some of her favourite music and try to distract her.

C. Join her in criticizing the other driver.

D. Tell her about a time something like this happened to you, and how angry you felt, until you saw the other driver was on the way to the hospital.

8. A discussion between you and your partner has escalated into a shouting match. You are both upset and, in the heat of the argument, have started making personal attacks which neither of you really mean. What is the best thing to do?

A. Agree to take a 20-minute break before continuing the discussion.

B. Go silent, regardless of what your partner says.

C. Say you are sorry, and ask your partner to apologize too.

D. Stop for a moment, collect your thoughts, then restate your side of the case as precisely as possible.

9. You have been given the task of managing a team that has been unable to come up with a creative solution to a work problem. What is the first thing that you do?

A. Draw up an agenda, call a meeting and allot a specific period of time to discuss each item.

B. Organize an off-site meeting aimed specifically at encouraging the team to get to know each other better.

C. Ask each person individually for ideas about how to solve the problem.

D. Have a brainstorming session, encouraging each person to say whatever comes to mind, no matter how wild.

10. You have recently been assigned a young manager in your team, and have noticed that he appears to be unable to make the simplest of decisions without seeking advice from you. What do you do?

A. Accept that he 'does not have what it take to succeed around here' and find others in your team to take on his tasks.

B. Get an HR manager to talk to him about where he thinks his future within the organization might lie.

C. Purposely give him lots of complex decisions to make so that he will become more confident in the role.

D. Engineer an ongoing series of challenging but manageable experiences for him, and make yourself available to act as his mentor.

Scoring

There are up to ten points available for each situation, as described below. So adding together the points for each of your answers will give you a score out of 100 – your EI percentage score.

1. The only answer which doesn't indicate emotional intelligence is D. It suggests a lack of awareness of what is going on. Attempts at managing your own emotions and being both vigilant and aware of how others are acting are important EI skills. **So you get 10 points for choosing either A, B or C.**

2. Answer A suggests an emotionally driven confrontation and a lack of skill by trying to get behaviour change through a public confrontation. Doing nothing (Answer C) would leave the problem unresolved and the potential resentment may fester and grow in the future. The solution for this one is to work collaboratively with the colleague in future but also to manage your own

feelings. **You get 5 points for choosing B and 10 points for D.**

3. An important part of emotional intelligence is sensitivity to others' feelings and a positive attitude towards helping both them and yourself to resolve difficulties. Showing that you understand the client's concerns but also helping him to feel that his concerns are being resolved would be the emotionally intelligent options. **5 points for B and 10 points for D.**

4. Failure at something almost always generates strong emotions and frequently guilt. In the short term, such emotions can overwhelm rational thinking and lead to skewed decision-making. Keeping control involves trying as hard as possible to use logic and analysis as well as accepting both our strengths and weaknesses. **A gets you 10 points and C scores 5 points.**

5. Racism is unacceptable in any situation. Ignoring it can seem like an endorsement. Whilst action subsequently might demonstrate your position, the emotionally intelligent person has a clear set of values, is confident in their own beliefs and prepared to speak up, even if their views are different. **So B scores 5 points, C scores 10 points and D also gets 5 points.**

6. Self-management is a core characteristic of emotional intelligence; it involves managing disruptive emotions and impulses. Being positive, resilient and focused are

characteristics of someone in control, so **B gets you 10 points and C is 5 points.**

7. Empathizing with someone who is in a state of emotional arousal is one of the best ways to mollify them. Attempting either to distract them or to minimize their concern is likely to lead to even stronger emotion being displayed and is unlikely to be effective. **C gets 5 points** for building empathy and making the colleague feel positive and accepted about her viewpoint. **D, however, gets 10 points** because in addition to empathy, you are giving your colleague a rational analysis and getting them to think of potential negative consequences for the bad driver. This engages cognitive processes to help reduce the level of emotion, showing good relationship management.

8. The emotionally intelligent person has two problems here, managing the partner's emotionality and managing their own. Time for a break. Continuing will make things worse. **A gets 10 points.**

9. Helping a team to work in a creative manner involves acknowledging the link between feelings and creative thinking. A team is only as good as the quality of relationships and ability to collaborate. So relationship management, finding ways to help people build on each others' work, and being non-traditional are required for this situation. **B gets 10 points; D gets 5 points.**

10. Empathy with a young manager in a new situation, together with the uncertainty of his decision-making, suggests a need for support and incremental building of confidence. Exposure and threat would merely build anxiety. Supporting him and challenging him at the same time are the best options for growth. **B scores 5 points and D gets 10 points.**

This questionnaire has been trialled recently with more than 200 people. The average score for 30- to 50-year-old participants was 65 and for younger people 60. Eleven per cent of the total group volunteered that they had problems with relationship management or self-awareness. There were no statistically significant differences between the scores for men and women

Ten questions cannot give you a comprehensive measure of your existing level of emotional intelligence, but this quiz was designed to give you a sense of the skills involved in emotionally intelligent behaviour and where some of your own strengths might lie.

The foundations of emotional intelligence

What is 'intelligence' anyway?
When you think about intelligence, what comes to mind? A short-sighted scientist perhaps, with nights spent huddled under a reading lamp or in front of a computer screen, doing abstract calculations long into the night? If you are

thinking along these lines, you are not alone. Alfred Binet developed the first IQ test in 1905 and measuring intelligence has been a preoccupation of psychologists ever since. Whilst these tests have been useful for predicting academic success, until recently they only measured someone's ability to handle information in the abstract – ignoring other skills or abilities. Research in 2002 suggested that this type of intelligence was responsible for less than 25 per cent of someone's chances of success in later life. A review of 52 studies in 1994 put the figure closer to 5 per cent – other factors accounting for the remaining 95 per cent. Whatever intelligence is, shouldn't these 'other factors' count?

Other views of intelligence have been proposed, including Thorndike in 1920, Kelly in the 1950s and Howard Gardner in 1983, all of whom challenged the idea of a single, problem-solving intelligence measured by classical IQ tests. They proposed that we have a number of different types of intelligence for dealing with others – which is often described as 'social' intelligence. This idea underpinned the work done over the 1980s and 90s (notably by John Mayer, Peter Salovey, David Caruso and Richard Boyatzis), and Reuven Bar-On coined the phrase 'an emotional intelligence' in a 1980 dissertation. Then came the smash hit of 1995, Daniel Goleman's bestselling book *Emotional Intelligence*.

The work before Goleman's book had focused on social or emotional intelligence as an innate ability, one of the key perspectives which some people take today. Goleman was a science journalist with experience in clinical psycho-therapy and meditational psychology. Now a leading management psychologist, he argues that there's more than an innate ability involved, using evidence garnered by, amongst others, David McClelland about the competences and behaviours of leaders and high performers in industry, commerce and the public sector.

Psychologists identify various forms of intelligence. Emotional intelligence incorporates at least two of them:

Cognitive intelligence – the ability to think rationally, act in a purposeful way and manage your environment. It's your intellectual, analytical, logical and rational skill set.

Social intelligence – the ability to understand and manage situations which involve other people. It is your ability to be aware of yourself, to understand yourself, to manage relationships and understand the emotional content of behaviour.

Researchers looking at both forms of intelligence have designed different ways of measuring emotional intelligence which demonstrate their perspectives. But there's a problem with measurement. Many ideas behind emotional intelligence, like managing your own emotions, are difficult to measure reliably and validly because of the subjective nature of emotional experiences. There are also many tests of the 'traits' view of EI (this is the view that says EI is merely a function of personality), which look essentially like traditional personality tests.

A question of culture – stoicism and the 'stiff upper lip'

Being stoical, the ultimate belief in the 'stiff upper lip', was difficult for ordinary human beings to live up to even in Ancient Greece, but it has been the prevailing idea in Western culture throughout most of history. **Stoics** argued that thinking, logic, intellect and reason were the only reliable ways of living. Creating structure and order in life were prized along with inner solitude, forbearance in adversity and the acceptance of fate. They believed that emotions stemmed from false judgements. Feelings were too idiosyncratic and subjective so an unreliable basis for living and working together.

Jean Martin Charcot linked emotion to hysteria in the late Victorian period; 'giving in to emotion' was seen as either a physical (convulsive) disorder or a psychological problem. Histories of psychology acknowledge that defining emotions in this way involved a pretty sexist perspective. For many years, the mainly male perspective was that emotion was a *female problem*.

In contrast, writer Georg Simmel saw urban and workplace life in the 1950s as a dangerous place to be. He pictured modern industrial life as an endless flow of impersonal stimulation, contrasting with the warmth of a village life more rooted in emotional connections. The village life, he argues, creates a sense of empowerment and purpose with good community relationships as a result. The typical modern view of life, Simmel claims, is 'blasé'. He suggests that the stiff upper lip was widespread across the twentieth century with 'reserve, coldness and indifference always in danger of turning into hatred.' It was in this context that research into emotional intelligence began.

In the US, the stiff-upper-lip approach was challenged – in the acceptance of 'therapy' and in some cases the 'touchy-feely' extremes of modern management. Both of these can be traced back to two periods in history: the years before the First World War and the 1960s.

Psychoanalysis found a resounding echo in the academic and clinical worlds, the newspapers, popular culture and in management after Freud spoke at Clark University in the USA (1909), and Jung's subsequent lectures (at Fordham University 1912 and in London 1913 and 1914). Newspapers supported the expansion of technology and the development of new ideas, including the "new science" of the mind. It was taken up almost as a social experiment by wealthy people and only gained credibility as the science of psychology matured. In the 1960s, movements like the California 'humanistic psychologies' rooted in social change and the Esalen Institute's human potentiality workshops also questioned the role which emotions played in human interaction.

Over the last 50 years, stoicism and emotional importance have ebbed and flowed often correlating with economic success. When times are tough, the stiff upper lip re-emerges. In 2012, the drivers for stiff-upper-lip behaviour continue. Levels of poverty may be very different to the nineteenth century but banking crises, recessions and economic instability over the last ten years have set an adversarial climate. Even after retirement, say older people's charities, many pensioners have to fight for recognition and the rights they are due. The media are often guilty of sensationalism and certainly both television and newspapers are constantly full of adversarial images depicting war, poverty and violence.

The idea of emotional intelligence affirms that, as social animals, we need to use our social and emotional skills to deal with others effectively. For some, the drivers may have changed but they will still be more comfortable avoiding dealing with feelings.

The stiff upper lip questionnaire
The following questionnaire is designed to assess the significance of the 'stiff upper lip' culture in your outlook. Below is a list of personal qualities. Decide how each quality applies to you – either positively or negatively and to what degree. For each one, you need to give yourself a score between minus 10 (the quality doesn't feature in your behaviour at all, ever!)

and plus 10 (it is very characteristic of how you behave, all the time). Write down your scores next to the qualities in the list. When you have completed the questionnaire to your satisfaction, look at the scoring information to get your stiff upper lip score.

Qualities

- Decisive
- Forceful
- Stubborn
- Restrained
- Cool
- Persistent
- Results-focused
- Dominant
- Resilient
- Strong personality

- Tough
- Demanding
- Strong
- Flexible
- Purposeful
- Powerful
- Risk taker
- Emphatic
- Challenging
- Cold

Scoring

Combine all your negative scores and all your positive scores. Subtract the negative from the positive to obtain your overall 'stiff upper lip' score.

Interpretation

140–200 (very high)

You have a rating in the top 10 per cent of stiff upper lips! You are probably really effective in crises or in situations where there is a need to push policies or ideas through against opposition. You will be most effective in situations which do not involve major change or when dealing with people who have little interest in taking any responsibility. People like you sometimes make successful entrepreneurs but, equally, many prefer to go into some other business, once their original start-up has begun to grow. They report that others may have difficulty opening up to them. Using your emotional intelligence will make working with you easier and help you deal with more motivated people in rapidly moving situations involving change.

95–139 (strong)
Thirty per cent of people doing this test score in the same range that you do. They tend to be assertive and success-ful people, but in organizations and situations where the culture is quite competitive. Many seem to be employed in sales occupations or as entrepreneurs. They also seem to have relationships (as opposed to acquaintances) which are either very long term or new and not very deep. Emotional intelligence can help you to further your understanding of others and build more open and loyal relationships.

0–94 (average)
Thirty per cent of people doing the test score similarly to you. They often describe themselves as people who have a sense of purpose and a clear image of themselves, and who enjoy team leadership roles. They are rated by others as independent and enjoyable to work with, without being

overly pushy. As with those who score strongly (above) they are sometimes seen to succumb to stress when the going is tough, sometimes not recognizing the effect of pressure on themselves. Emotional intelligence can help you to become self-aware, understand others, manage your stress and build better long-term relationships.

Below 0 (low)
Thirty per cent of people have negative scores. They seem to be people who are less confident in situations where they act alone and other tests suggest that they may doubt their own abilities, particularly in decision-making, setting personal goals and 'persistence' (carrying through projects). On the other hand, many people with these scores seem to be skilled communicators who value working with others. Emotional intelligence can help you to think through your own feelings and approach and help you become more assertive about your own values and priorities.

Using your stiff upper lip score
The earlier descriptions of emotional intelligence and stoic behaviour are not intended to promote one and devalue the other. Neither should be thought of as the only skill set needed. There are many situations in which strong and independent character is important. But emotional intelligence is an essential requirement where there is a need to work with, influence and seek cooperation with other people. It is a complement to stoicism and strength of character.

So just watch out for extreme scores in this question-naire. Anything above 140 suggests you may make much less use of emotional intelligence than situations require.

Emotions and emotional intelligence

You don't need to be a psychologist to understand emotional intelligence. But an important part of the foundation for EI is an awareness that our emotions are hard-wired into the brain – and that there is a purpose for them.

What is emotion? A feeling? Then what is a feeling? These terms are difficult to define and even more difficult to understand completely. People have been attempting to understand the phenomenon for thousands of years. Over that time, there has been a wide range of scientific opinion regarding the nature and importance of emotions. Some psychologists have felt that the idea of emotion is unnecessary – behaviour is the central issue and stimulus or threat produces instinctual responses. Others believe that ideas about arousal or 'activation' are less confusing than complex theories of emotion and development. Some psychologists maintain that emotion is the body's primary motivational system, a visceral function of the organs triggered by the autonomic nervous system, whilst others say human beings are essentially rational beings – our 'reason for being' is essentially cognitive/intellectual and it's our logic and judgment that is core.

Whatever the truth of these ideas, people surround themselves with people and objects to which they become emotionally attached, and for many people the 'reason for being' is the warmth of that attachment. Most psychologists acknowledge the immense power emotions have to shape our understanding, our ways of thinking, the decisions we take and the habits or attitudes we adopt. Cognitive science has repeatedly demonstrated the role that emotion plays in decision-making, to the extent that if logic and feeling point in different directions, most people go with their instincts.

In everyday life, people universally experience the difficulties of both coping with their own emotions and the practical difficulties created by those of others. Emotional disorders affect huge numbers of people. In 2010, the UK government estimated that 15 per cent of people will have a bout of severe depression at some point in their lives (women are twice as likely to suffer from depression as men, although men are far more likely to commit suicide). Two per cent of teenagers in the UK are diagnosed with emotional disorders before the age of eighteen; and emotional disorders in old age is also a major, and increasing, problem. Emotional intelligence is important for our own mental health and gives us the capacity to understand both ourselves and how we deal with the pressures we face.

PART I: THE EMOTIONAL INTELLIGENCE FRAMEWORK

The emotional intelligence framework outlined in this part of the book is intended for busy people who want to develop EI but may not have the opportunity to trawl through heaps of heavyweight literature.

The framework describes the four interrelated elements central to an emotionally intelligent approach. These determine how effectively you can understand and interact with other people. Each of these elements involves a wide range of ideas and skills. As well as enhancing your performance, understanding and putting them into practice will have an effect on the mood and sense of comfort you have when dealing with people. Stated simply, the key components are:

1. Self-knowledge
2. Managing your emotions
3. Understanding others' behaviours and feelings
4. Managing your relationships (using effective social skills).

Let's now look at each of these in more detail.

1. Self-knowledge

Understanding yourself is probably the starting point for emotional intelligence; it provides a foundation for managing yourself, spotting emotions in others and managing the relationships in that situation. When someone mentions self-awareness, the first thing you might think about is how your behaviour affects other people and what they think of you. 'Seeing ourselves as others see us' is a mantra heard again and again in relation to communication skills, negotiating, staff management, politics and the media for many years. But what does it mean?

---

1. Think of a person you know and the situations in which you meet them. What are they like? Write a short description.

2. Look at the description you have written. How many different factors have you written about? What are the key perspectives that help you to form your opinion about them?

Self-awareness is about understanding ourselves and knowing what pushes our buttons and why.

Our past and our self-image play a large part in how we choose to interpret other people's behaviour. More

34

importantly they also determine the way we act and the effect we have on others.

When we look at other people, we observe many aspects which shape our perceptions of them. First impressions are important because they influence the way we interpret others' initial behaviour. These might be based on the manner of the initial contact, their physical appearance, dress, friendliness, manners, accent and many other characteristics.

We all have our own individual behaviours, which shape the judgements people make about us. Such behaviours often stem from our backgrounds or demonstrate what we value. Some of these behaviour-forming factors are:

- The lessons we learned, both as children and later in life, about what is acceptable

- Our needs for affection, warmth or closeness (or coolness, distance and formality)

- The beliefs and principles we hold about ourselves, the way life is, and about other people

- The type of instincts or 'inner voice' that gives us insights or tells us what is important

- Our 'cognitive strategies' – ways of thinking which determine comfort or discomfort with people and things

- The lifestyle we seek

- The way we want to be seen by others

- The goals we have and our sense of purpose

- The things we dismiss, reject or find difficult to deal with.

It would be great to think of ourselves or others as free agents determining who we are and what we do. Emotional intelligence can help with that. But most of our inner drive, and certainly the way we react to others, comes from our own past experiences. The authority figures we have encountered, our parents or grandparents, the role models we have created and the managers we have worked for – they have all played a role in moulding and conditioning who we are and the effect we create on others. So too does the way we react to the emotions we experience.

 Self-awareness is about understanding ourselves and knowing what pushes our buttons and why.

Our past and our self-image play a large part in how we choose to interpret other people's behaviour. More importantly, it also determines the way we act and the effect we have on others.

Mindfulness and understanding our emotions

Have you ever driven to work and, when you've arrived, cannot remember your journey? Or spent a morning serving customers and have difficulty later recalling what happened? Being on automatic pilot reduces our conscious engagement with what we are doing and there are risks attached. You don't want to be in front of a driver on automatic pilot, nor to be served by someone who is not paying attention to what you need.

But being in the 'mindless' state of automatic pilot opens you up to other problems. You can become prone to old habits and behaviours, perhaps leaving people feeling you aren't interested in them. Events and situations around you can trigger old feelings and sensations which become barriers and make your mood worsen. And we can fail to notice important signals from the people we are dealing with, which suggest we had better do something differently and straight away.

By becoming more aware of our thoughts, feelings and bodily sensations as they happen, we are creating the basis of greater freedom and choice in how we act and the opportunity to be more responsive to others. We don't have to go into the same habits or mental tramlines which have caused problems in the past and we can choose to act differently – perhaps building more effective relationships or coping with stresses better.

What this means, of course, is that we may also need to develop another dimension to our problem-solving approach. Most of us have developed, to a greater or lesser extent, a set of critical thinking tools to fix problems. Analytical thinking, problem-solving and judgement are vitally important for an emotionally intelligent person. But problems in relationships, with emotions or with our own unconscious reactions to things, may not respond in the same way as a logistics or resourcing problem.

So what extra skills do you need to deal with people in a mindful or self-aware manner? Try reflecting on your own experience:

 When you are in a discussion that you find difficult, when do you become aware of the following? Give yourself a score between 1 and 5 (1 = immediately, 5 = days later, or not at all).

Recognizing the emotions you experience _____

The need to relax your body when you feel tense _____

How agitated you have become _____

The need to do something about the stress you feel _____

The need to communicate empathy _____

That others are not sharing your ideas and goals _____

The need to gain others' commitment _____

How positive or negative you are being _____

The need to change course to develop motivation _____

The need to show your sense of humour _____

How well did you do? The most important aspect of the exercise is whether you are conscious of what you are feeling, as it happens. So if you scored lots of 5s you are like many people – doing things and reflecting afterwards. You need to develop your sensitivity about what's happening now so you can respond there and then. Problems of unclear goals are best picked up straight away. When people are feeling uncertain or vulnerable, they need empathy then, not later.

Mindfulness means paying attention on purpose to what is happening in the present moment, without judging whether it is right or wrong. It emphasizes a collaborative way of working and draws on your listening skills. You also need to control your own emotions, so you can 'hear' what's going on.

Part of mindfulness is knowing what you are feeling as it happens. Being able to give the emotion you experience a name is not some touchy-feely idea about sensitivity. Naming it involves consciously thinking about what is happening and choosing how to react. It gives you the capacity to both register its impact (which engages your limbic system) and also trigger control through greater involvement of other parts of the brain (cognitive structures).

This balance of thought and emotion gives you more control of the feelings you experience by engaging different structures in the brain. Mindfulness is an important element in emotional intelligence because it increases awareness and provides better control. It lets you know when your approach to dealing with others is getting skewed.

 Read the list below and think about whether you tend to do these things. If you do, how frequently does it happen?

- Unconsciously ignore or push feelings, problems or difficulties out of my mind.

- Behave in ways that do not match the way I really think or feel.

- Become childlike or defensive.

- Rationalize away things that make me feel bad or unsatisfied.

- Take out my feelings on other people.

- Represent my own thoughts or feelings as the thoughts or feelings of others.

Describing your emotions

As mentioned above, being able to identify and name your emotions as they arise is an important part of mindfulness.

If you can find words to describe how you feel at the time, and (even better) what's causing it, you will automatically become more sensitive and aware. Doing this will provide options for you:

- You may decide that you do not want to feel that way.

- You may decide that your feelings are about things in your past rather than the situation at hand.

- You may begin to think, more tangibly, what it is that others have done to make you feel this way.

- You may begin to think about other people's feelings too.

When we think about our own feelings, we can often gauge how strongly we feel them by our choice of words.

The list below illustrates the wide variety of words people use to describe emotions; all these terms are used to label the emotions arising from just one feeling – confusion. Note the way the strength of feelings is expressed by using different words:

Strong feeling: Baffled, chaotic, confused, flustered, rattled, shaken up, startled, stumped, stunned, thrown, thunderstruck, trapped.

Medium feeling: Puzzled, blurred, disquieted, foggy, frustrated, misled, mixed up, perplexed, troubled.

Slight feeling: Distracted, uncertain, uncomfortable, undecided, unsure.

Researchers differ about whether there is a definitive list of emotions and whether some are more fundamental than others. Either way, with such a wide selection of terms, it is easy to see why defining emotions can be difficult. But being able to put a name to the feelings you experience helps you to stay in control of yourself. Choosing and using words to describe how you feel at any given point actually helps to engage different parts of the brain from those primarily used for emotion and reaction. (There is more information about this in Chapter 7, 'Emotional Intelligence and Health'.)

Try to think of what's underneath your feelings too. For example, a feeling of being annoyed might actually result from a feeling of inferiority: 'I am *irritated* when my boss uses long words. I use straightforward words. He makes me feel *inferior*. It's not fair, my ideas are as good as his.' Naming your underlying feelings can also help you to understand yourself and what you might need to keep in control.

The emotional chain

To understand the process that leads to the way we feel and react, think about the following scenario:

You are walking through an unlit park late one night. You hear footsteps behind you. You notice your heart begins to beat faster and you begin to tremble. Your breathing quickens and you are aware of the dark shadows moving near you. You just know that something is about to happen. You are feeling frightened and begin to run …

Four mental and physiological processes were involved in that situation:

Arousal   Interpretation   Stimulation   Behaviour

What was the order in which you think they might have happened?

There are several well-known ideas about the process involved in generating feelings and emotions. In the main, they describe a sequence which involves noticing (sometimes very small) things which trigger thinking about their significance or meaning. Depending on whether the meaning is perceived as positive or negative, changes in brain chemistry alert the body for any physical activity which may be necessary – for example in the situation described above, the 'fight or flight' needed for survival. We notice our bodies as they change.

It is at this point that we become aware of feeling something – curiosity or fear, happiness or irritation – linked to the physical change. This knowledge in turn generates further thinking about what to do and how to react.

If you chose stimulation followed by interpretation, then arousal and behaviour, your answer would agree with mainstream ideas about how emotions influence our reactions.

Tuning in to how you are feeling

There are many things going on right now, stimuli surrounding you in your immediate environment, sensations in your body, and thoughts and feelings in your mind of which you probably were not consciously aware.

Have you been paying attention to the room you are in? Stop for a moment and close your eyes when you reflect on the following questions:

- What is the temperature?
- How does it smell?
- What are you sitting on?
- Is it comfortable?

And your body:
- Do you have any aches or pains?
- Are your muscles tight or relaxed?
- Is your stomach pleasantly full or is it painfully empty?

Reflect on the following questions:
- What thoughts have been occupying your mind in the last couple of minutes?
- Where has that taken you outside the room?

Becoming aware of and understanding your feelings

The self-awareness exercise above is intended to make you think about how many triggers there are for our feelings, thoughts and perceptions. But self-awareness is more than paying attention thoroughly. It is changing *how* we pay attention.

Most people would say that they pay attention to things around them – and of course we do, if only to get things done that we need to. Usually we perceive things through a sort of 'tunnel vision'. If we have been chronically unhappy, for instance, we tend to see things through that prism. And with a particular problem in mind, anything that doesn't immediately seem relevant drops out of our field of view.

Real awareness asks you to turn a switch, focusing on 'What's going on inside me at this moment?' It means suspending judgement for a time and putting your goals in the back seat while you describe what is *actually going on* rather than what you *think should* be.

Being open means turning off the switch marked 'autopilot' in which we tend to operate for long periods. This gives you a more vivid sense of the situation and helps you notice the clues which tell you about how other people are feeling or reacting to you. You experience things you may never have noticed before and become more aware of whether your usual reactions are appropriate. Mindfulness can transform the way you understand situations and give you many more options for how you react to them.

Accurate self-assessment involves:
- Knowing your own strengths, weaknesses and limitations
- Being open to what is happening around you
- Valuing feedback
- Having a sense of humour and perspective
- The capacity to reflect and to learn from experience
- Being open to change.

Being open to new experience

In the last section, we began to identify both the effect and the risks of operating on autopilot. Self-awareness helps you to operate in a conscious, non-judgemental, *switched-on* way. We also need to limit autopilot behaviour for another reason – doing so opens the way for us to experience something we haven't been aware of before.

Our reactions are often based on significant events and interactions of the past; they are models of behaviours, feelings and options constructed for us to draw on to deal with new situations. A significant part of this 'map' is developed during our early lives and is largely determined by the people and situations we have experienced. We often act from the map rather than the reality of the situation. Mindfulness, being aware of what is going on around you, helps to stop you going on to autopilot and opens the way for you to see new possibilities. We can change old behaviours that didn't achieve what we wanted, or find different ways to react that will make others respond positively. We can also respond in ways that make us feel better about the overall situation.

A sense of optimism

Would you describe yourself as an *optimist* or a *pessimist*? People differ in how they describe themselves because they have different *expectations* about future events. Take the achievement of personal goals and the benefits you will accrue. Optimists are generally confident about the future and are characterized by a belief that outcomes will be positive. Pessimists have a generalized sense of doubt, are often hesitant and perhaps cynical about future outcomes, perhaps believing that 'no expectation means no disappointment'. Past disappointment can lead to fearing the future.

Optimism is better than pessimism

Research in the field of positive psychology has found many advantages to taking an optimistic perspective, such as:

- Optimists adapt better when they experience negative life events, for example they have better survival and/or recovery rates for coronary bypass surgery, bone marrow transplants, breast cancer and Aids.

- They experience less distress when dealing with difficulties in their lives, resulting in lower rates of depression and anxiety.

- Optimism is a valuable framework when coping with problems. It is conducive to humour, identifying possibilities and visualizing the problem differently. As a coping skill it enables you to accept the inevitable and learn for future events. It is a more effective coping skill than pessimism.

- Optimists stick their head in the sand *less* than pessimists, perhaps surprisingly. They respond to health warnings more quickly and catch serious problems earlier than pessimists (who often try to distance themselves from problems).

- Optimists appear to have greater 'stickability' than pessimists, who (perhaps anticipating failure) give up more quickly.

- Optimistic assumptions tend to provide more flexible responses.

Is there a downside?

Optimists can sometimes downplay risks with the result that they are more likely to participate in dangerous activities. I'm not sure how many pessimists are likely to go bungee jumping! Perhaps we would be better off with a mix of pessimism and optimism in this regard. In dealing with others, however, emotional intelligence is much more a characteristic of optimists than of pessimists.

There are a number of strategies to counter pessimistic styles of thinking. A key strategy is to work on the way we explain the causes and influence of positive and negative events.

The three explanations for optimism

There are three explanations which illustrate the way optimists differ from pessimists; they relate to whether the events are construed as **permanent or temporary, global or specific** and caused **internally or externally**. The following examples illustrate the different outlooks they generate:

Setbacks are seen by *low-optimism* people as:
- Permanent
- All-pervasive
- Personal.

They are seen by *high-optimism* people as:
- Temporary
- Specific to the situation
- Caused by external events.

Success is seen by *low-optimism* people as:
- Temporary
- Specific to the situation
- Rooted in external factors.

It is seen by *high-optimism* people as:
- Permanent
- Having widespread significance
- Deriving from the people involved.

Long-term issues (such as difficulty making presentations) are explained by *low-optimism* people as:

'I always find presentations difficult.'

They are explained by *high-optimism* people as:

'I sometimes find presentations a bit tough.'

Problems in handling awkward situations are explained by *low-optimism* people as:

'I dislike handling awkward situations.'

They are explained by *high-optimism* people as:

'I didn't handle that situation well.'

Personal achievement (such as sales success) is explained by *low-optimism* people as:

'This is an easy product to sell.'

It is explained by *high-optimism* people as

'I've really been putting in extra effort.'

Positive psychologist Martin Seligman argues that we can acquire 'learned optimism', mitigating the negative impact of a more pessimistic attitude by challenging the way we think about things.

Seligman believes that psychology should explore strengths as well as weakness. Having worked extensively with depressed patients who had acquired what he describes as 'learned helplessness', he went on to develop his concept of 'learned optimism'. In research undertaken in the insurance industry, Seligman and his colleagues found that optimists who were employed as new salesmen sold 37 per cent more insurance in their first two years than pessimists.

When the company then hired a special group of individuals who scored high on optimism even though they did not have the normal experience required in sales jobs, they outsold the more experienced pessimists by 21 per cent in their first year and even more in the second.

Challenging your own pessimistic thinking means asking yourself:

• What evidence is there for your negative thoughts?

• Is your pessimistic thinking related to past events? Have things changed now?

• Can you find an alternative explanation or other evidence for the situation?

• Even if there is no positive explanation, does it really matter?

• What are the implications of the situation?

• Is it really damaging?

• And if you can't find an optimistic explanation for the cause, which perspective would be more helpful for your mood?

REMEMBER THIS!!! Optimism is often a *consequence* of EI. It is about, when things go wrong, tending to see the causes as specific, temporary and linked to factors outside yourself.

Optimism involves accurate self-awareness and the ability to be take control of anxieties and frustrations – and to manage interactions in a way which lessens stress rather than succumbs to it.

Pessimists are less likely to have these characteristics. Unlike optimists, they also tend to see causes as widespread or even universal, permanent and often resulting from internal weaknesses.

There's more on the benefits of optimism and empathy in Chapter 5, 'EI and the workplace'.

Self-esteem and confidence

Everyone holds opinions about the type of person they are and how they relate to others. These opinions are at the heart of your self-esteem and they affect how you feel about and value yourself.

Self-esteem is not static or fixed. The beliefs you hold about yourself can change throughout your life and events like redundancy or a relationship breaking up may give your confidence a huge knock. If you have high self-esteem, you will generally see yourself in a positive light. High self-esteem can help you bounce back, acting as a buffer increasing your resilience. Someone with low self-esteem will often have built up negative beliefs about themselves, focusing on things they see as weaknesses, and experiencing feelings such as anxiety as a result.

The types of belief which have developed, often since childhood, make the difference between high and low self-esteem. If the beliefs are mainly negative, there is evidence that they can put you at a higher risk of mental health problems including depression and mood disorders. Low self-esteem and confidence are closely related to your mood and self-image, so it is important to realize that beliefs are only opinions, they are not facts. They can be biased or inaccurate, and there are steps you can take to change them.

USEFUL TIP If you feel that working on your self-esteem might be useful, you could try keeping a thought diary or record for a few weeks. Write down details of situations, how you felt, particularly when your self-esteem was low, and what you think your underlying belief was. As you identify the core beliefs you hold about yourself, you can begin to challenge and change them.

What causes low self-esteem?

There are no universal causes of low self-esteem because your development so far is likely to have been a highly individual process. Your personality and any inherited characteristics will play a part and your experiences and relationships are important. Negative experiences in childhood are often particularly damaging to self-esteem. In your early years your personality and sense of self is being formed, and harmful experiences can leave you feeling that you are not valued or important. You have not had a chance to build up any resilience, so this negative view can become what you believe about yourself.

Negative core beliefs about your intelligence, appearance and abilities are often formed by experiences such as the following:

- Having your physical and emotional needs neglected in childhood
- Failing to meet the expectations of your parents
- Feeling like the 'odd one out' at school
- Being subject to abuse – sexual, emotional or physical – and the loss of control associated with this
- Social isolation and loneliness.

Poor self-esteem is also fed by a vicious circle of experience: you learn to expect the worst and when you think it is beginning to happen, you react badly because at the back of your mind, all the time, you are feeling anxious. You might shake, blush or panic, or behave in a way that you think will keep you 'safe', e.g. shy or vulnerable people who do not go to social events on their own. This 'security behaviour' is likely to confirm the negative core beliefs you have about yourself. This adds to your store of examples, leaving you feeling you have even less chance of coping next time. It is a cycle that might seem unbreakable.

Strengthening self-esteem
The following tips can be really helpful. Keep checking on them during the day. They should keep you positive and engaged in boosting your self-esteem:

1. Stop comparing yourself to other people.
2. Don't put yourself down.
3. Get into the habit of thinking and saying positive things about you to yourself.
4. Accept compliments.
5. Use self-help books and websites to help you change your beliefs.
6. Spend time with positive, supportive people.
7. Acknowledge your positive qualities and things you are good at.
8. Be assertive; don't allow people to treat you with a lack of respect.
9. Be helpful and considerate to others.
10. Engage in work and hobbies that you enjoy.

We have seen that your self-esteem comes from core beliefs about your value as a person. If you want to increase your emotional intelligence, you need to challenge and change negative beliefs. This might feel like an impossible task, but there are a lot of different ways that you can do it. A critical issue is having a strong sense of purpose and direction, as explained in the next section.

Purpose and direction

People with strong emotional intelligence are often seen as independent characters, not afraid to question what is happening and with a value set which they are happy to share and discuss. Similarly, they have a clear sense of direction, which they are also upfront about.

 What do you want to achieve in your life or your career, and what are your plans for achieving it?

With that in mind, think about the following questions:
- What sort of reaction do you think is likely if you are seen by others as passive or indifferent?
- What do you consider the consequences might be if you were unable to voice views that are different or challenging, perhaps unpopular even?
- And what sort of reaction might you receive if you are seen by others as indecisive or you freeze whenever things are uncertain?

Answer: You are unlikely to achieve respect or impact on others very easily!

The self-knowledge aspect of emotional intelligence is concerned with understanding the way we try to gain the trust of others and influence them. Good self-awareness includes knowing the strengths and weaknesses you have – the behaviours you are skilled in and those you need to develop to become more effective. Crucially, it involves thinking carefully about what you want to achieve and whether you can balance your drive to organize things (systems, procedures and tasks) with the importance of the emotional side of the enterprise.

Acting purposefully

Knowing your strengths and weaknesses can be a major step in both personal confidence and effective communication. Knowing where you stand and having a clear set of values or beliefs are also pre-requisites for confidence and impact. The sense of grounding and self-confidence that these qualities can give you was described many years before emotional intelligence was known as such, by Pitt the Younger in his description of what a committed minister of the crown needs to be. Pitt said, 'I like knowing where I stand, being able to be honest about what I think, comfortable with how I feel and genuine about what I say … When you go into a bear pit like the House of Commons you may have a vision for the future but you feel as though you have both feet planted on the same ground that ordinary people walk.'

A sense of purpose, driven by values, is a powerful force. The impact it can create is illustrated by Japanese ceramics technology manufacturer Kyocera. Its founder, Kazuo Inamori, believes that 'the active force in any aspect of the business is people … they have their own will, mind, way of thinking. If they are not motivated to challenge, there will simply be no growth, no gain in productivity, no technological development.' His vision was to tap the potential of his staff with a corporate motto: 'Respect Heaven and Love People'. The impact that his beliefs have created, far from being overly romantic in a business world, has seen Kyocera going from start-up to £2 billion sales in 30 years, borrowing almost no money and achieving profit levels which are the envy of bankers worldwide.

Emotional intelligence underpinned the vision which drove Inamori and all his staff. The vision was that the urge to build something – to create – resides in us all. The juxtaposition of vision and current reality generated what Kyocera describes as 'creative tension which everyone enjoys trying to resolve'. The emotionally intelligent approach adopted was to ensure that everyone could share in the vision of trying to create. Senior management ensured that controls, limitations and constraints were kept to the minimum possible.

What is the sense of purpose which drives you in your work or personal life? Does your vision fill you with excitement and confidence? How well do the other people you relate to share your beliefs and excitement?

Expressing emotions

How do you feel when you ask someone to do something for you, which they might refuse? For many of us, this is a very difficult verbal exercise. We need to ask in such a way as to hopefully get the other person to comply, which involves ensuring the request is clear, specific and direct. On the other hand, if we are too direct, we may offend the person and reduce the likelihood of co-operation.

How we go about it is important. You might think that things get easier if the person is in a good mood. It seems sensible, but studies also suggest that our approach is more often determined by *our own* mood. Happy people interpreted situations more optimistically than others. They expressed themselves in more direct, sometimes impolite ways ('Just do it, will you!'). Less happy people used more formal, polite forms of request. And in complex situations with more demanding and difficult requests, this 'mood effect' was magnified.

Emotional intelligence requires an awareness of how emotion influences our thinking, judgement and interpersonal behaviours. In some situations we may need to deal with sensitive issues, in others with sensitive people. Our own emotion affects how we think, make decisions and communicate with others. In some cases, the situation may require us to talk about people's feelings or to confront the way in which they affect us. Communicating about emotion is not necessarily straightforward.

THINK ABOUT IT

Talking about feelings

On a scale of 1–10, how comfortable do you consider yourself to be talking about your own emotions (where 1 means you find it incredibly difficult, 10 means you do it all the time)?

Using a similar scale, how easy do you find discussing other people's emotions?

What is the worst situation you could imagine in which you would have to discuss emotions?

What is the most comfortable situation you can imagine in which to discuss emotions?

In the day-to-day situations you experience, how aware are you of the influence that your own emotions play?

The effect of emotions on thinking

Emotions have a multi-faceted impact on everything we think and do. Any decision you make may be driven by rational analysis of evidence, use of logic and analysis of data, but that isn't all. Most decisions also involve per-sonal values, the lessons of your experience, the potential impact your decision may have on others. If there are conflicts between thinking and feeling, it's usually the things we understood emotionally that people respond to. Our capacity to rationalize emotional decisions as logic is testament to the power of our emotions.

Moods

Unlike more intense emotions, moods are relatively low-intensity, diffuse and potentially pervasive states of mind. Everyday moods, whether good or bad, tend to colour our levels of optimism, relationships, achievements and pretty well everything we do. Their effect on how we might behave also can be more insidious, subtle and long-lasting.

For example, underlying low mood for many people can trigger stress responses in which they:

- Unconsciously push anxiety-producing information out of their own awareness

- React in a way contrary to how they actually think or feel

- Go back to an earlier stage of their development, perhaps behaving in a very dependent or childlike way

- Convince themselves that there is an acceptable reason for their behaviour when the real motive was unacceptable

- Redirect behaviour or emotion to a less threatening object (taking out frustrations, for example, on innocent objects or people)

- Project their own, often unacceptable, attitudes, perceptions, beliefs or feelings unfairly on to others.

Both our moods and our more intense emotions create filters through which we communicate and manage our relationships with others. When we act on autopilot, the stress reactions listed above help to remove short-term pressure but can create more significant problems, particularly for the individual involved. If the mood or emotional state continues, it can have a serious effect on the way we process information, see opportunities and perceive risk. It can become self-defeating and reinforce underlying negative emotional 'schemas' or patterns which, in turn, filter the way we perceive and process information.

Underlying patterns often found in people with low mood (more so when more severe depression is identified) are often described as 'life scripts'. These may include beliefs such as 'I need to depend on someone stronger than myself'; 'I can't change anything'; 'Only bad things happen to me'.

Positive and negative emotions and outlook
People experiencing positive emotions:
- Are likely to think well of others
- Expect to be accepted by others
- Are positive about their aspirations
- Are not afraid of others' reactions
- Work harder for people who demand higher standards
- Feel more comfortable with talented people

- Are comfortable defending themselves against negative comments by others.

Whereas people experiencing negative emotions:
- Are more likely to disapprove of others and themselves
- Expect rejection
- Have lower expectations and are more negative
- Are sensitive and perform poorly under scrutiny
- Work harder for uncritical, less demanding people
- Feel threatened easily
- Are more easily influenced and find defending themselves difficult.

As we have said before, self-knowledge, for emotionally intelligent people, helps us to understand ourselves and our way of thinking. We need to be aware when some of these problems are affecting us and the way they may skew our thinking. We need to be vigilant of any tendency towards:

- Over-generalizing
- Filtering out important things
- Discounting positives
- Absence of balance ('all or nothing' thinking)
- Jumping to conclusions
- Magnifying or minimizing problems
- Being judgemental
- Stereotyping people and situations
- Inability to detach ourselves from personal views.

Stress

Your reaction to stress

Coping with changing markets, juggling tasks, meeting difficult targets and dealing with difficult people – these are common difficulties which people have to cope with. Outside the workplace, relationship problems, bringing up children and healthcare issues need to be handled. When people believe they can't cope, stress is the result. It is another example of the pervasive influence emotions have on our thinking and behaviour. Emotionally intelligent people need to find ways of handling it, both for themselves and when the symptoms are shown by others.

A questionnaire included in Chapter 7, 'Emotional Intelligence and Health', can help you to form an idea of how prone to stress you are – see page 201.

Extreme stress and anxiety produce what eminent psychologist Jerry Suls calls a dangerous 'neurotic cascade' which can seriously limit your ability to use your emotional intelligence. The neurotic cascade refers to the destabilizing effect of negative thoughts and negative feelings clashing together to diminish your ability to cope. In this state, minor problems become magnified out of all proportion. Over-dramatizing negative outcomes – or 'awfulization' – and questions about coping are sometimes complemented with mood changes. In turn, these result in skewed thinking and further stress. Emotionally intelligent individuals recognize these problems and use effective strategies to tolerate stress. Effective coping strategies enable you to judge what a tolerable level is for yourself, and also for other people.

But some people seem to thrive on this type of situation. Look at the diagram below. Moving from left to right, the bold black line shows the impact of an increasing amount of stress. To begin with, the amount of stress being experienced is not enough to stimulate effective performance. Sometimes people find themselves in situations which give them insufficient stimulation or challenge to be worthwhile.

Tipping point

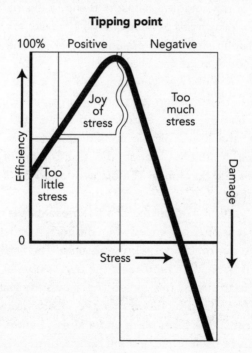

There comes a point shortly after that in which the optimum amount of stress is reached – the buzz of being busy, the challenge of a stretching but achievable target, the satisfaction of getting a new job under your belt.

Somewhere, and it differs for individuals, there comes a tipping point at which targets become unachievable, challenges just can't be met and the stress which was enabling becomes too much. As the amount of stress experienced increases even more, it becomes *disabling* and increases the risk of physiological damage. Being in this part of the model for prolonged periods of time increases the correlation between stress, depression and the immune system, and serious damage can occur.

Stress is a physical symptom, and not a root cause of problems. The situation (or stressor), in which challenges become unmanageable, causes the so-called 'fight or flight' reaction; the brain's limbic system activates the body's resistance to threat through the distribution of neurochemicals and hormones. The diagram opposite illustrates the process.

The vertical axis on the chart represents the level of physical tension experienced when the body is under attack, while the horizontal axis represents time. The flat horizontal line in the middle represents the body's normal level of resistance to stress. The curved line shows the increase in tension (measured by blood pressure, heart rate, vascular change, etc.) that takes place under stress, before, usually, stability is re-established and the body returns to normal.

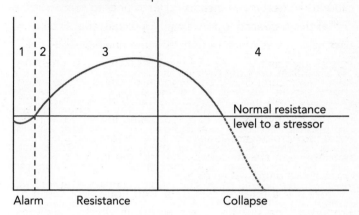

Key: 1 Shock
      2 Countershock
      3 Resistance
      4 Stabilization/Collapse

The body's reaction is made up of the following stages:

1. Shock: Realization of the nature of the situation and its demands creates an instant shock, creating confusion, uncertainty and a loss of visual and cognitive focus. At this stage, people tend to react automatically, although an alternative in some severe situations (particularly facing aggression) is that people freeze, becoming unable to respond.

2. Counter-shock: Upon realizing that we are at risk and may not be able to cope, the fight or flight response is triggered and catecholamines (including adrenaline, noradrenaline and dopamine) are released.

3. Resistance: The catecholamines affect the body in a number of ways, increasing blood flow, oxygenating the muscles, evacuating the digestive system, increasing visual and aural acuity, and increasing sensitivity to temperature. All of this is geared towards making us better able to combat risk.

4. Stabilization/Collapse: As the risk or threat abates the body should return to its normal state, controlled by the actions of our 'parasympathetic' system – a branch of the autonomic nervous system designed to re-establish equilibrium. However, depending on the level of the stress reaction, or if the fight or flight mechanism is being triggered too frequently, this stage can result in collapse rather than stabilizing at the normal resistance level. This creates a risk of tissue and organ damage, which can result in digestive tract problems, ulcerative colitis, triggering or worsening depression and cardiovascular disease, and speeding the progression of HIV/Aids.

But why are some people apparently immune to stress whilst others in the same situation experience disabling physical and psychological effects?

The two things that cause the sympathetic system (fight and flight response) to activate are:

- Firstly, the stressor itself: these are the characteristics of a situation that create anxiety, like pressure, excessive demands, personal threat or excessive risk.

- Secondly, the judgement that is made by the individual about the threat, based on their personality and experience: whether or not they feel able to cope. The immediate cause of stress is the perception of being out of control, being unable to prevent what may be seen as untoward consequences taking place.

The difference between coping and not coping is in large part due to the judgement of threat – two people faced with the same situation evaluate it differently. Another factor which affects the severity of stress is the coping behaviour used. It is important to recognize that not all options for coping with stress are helpful. Resorting to alcohol, smoking and excessive eating, for example, may make you feel better for a time but eventually do harm. This is adapting your behaviour to the stress but in a harmful way (so-called maladaptive response). Relaxing is often advocated – though not easy to do if you are coping with emotionally charged situations. Physical exercise and confronting problems are also often recommended as more positive adaptive behaviour.

People make choices about how they deal with stress, finding ways of coping, which, if removing the stressor isn't possible, enable them to adapt their behaviour to retain a positive perspective: this is vital both for working with others and for securing your own health and welfare. Some examples of both positive and negative adaptive behaviours are shown below:

Stressor	Adaptive behaviour
Overwork	Delegates some responsibility
Uncertainty of policy/ situation	Finds out what policy/situation is
Poor working relationship	Raises issue with colleague and negotiates better relationship
Poor career progression	Leaves organization for another
Organization versus family	Negotiates with boss more family time
Role ambiguity	Seeks clarification with colleagues or superior

Stressor	Maladaptive behaviour
Overwork	Accepts overload and general performance deteriorates
Uncertainty of policy/ situation	Guesses inappropriately
Poor relationship with colleague	Attacks colleague indirectly through third party
Poor career progression	Loses confidence and becomes convinced of own inadequacy
Organization versus family	Blames organization/individuals for problems/discontent
Role ambiguity	Becomes reactive/uncertain/ sows confusion

2. Managing your emotions

Our view of ourselves, our confidence, self-esteem, sense of purpose and awareness of the way we tend to react to things provides the basis for self-management, i.e. the ability to stay flexible and behave in a positive and effective way, appropriate to the situation you are in.

Self-awareness is one part of the balance between yourself and others which is at the heart of emotional intelligence. It provides an important insight into your needs and motivation when you are dealing with others. On its own, however, simply knowing how you feel does not lead to achieving your hopes and goals – in fact, it can actually cause you more problems than you might think. Take Janet, for example:

Janet is a fairly sensitive individual who has been experiencing some major life problems. She thinks of herself as relatively self-aware and in the situation described in the flow chart on page 72, Janet is probably thinking a lot about herself. What do you think the effect of this would be?

As we go through life, the challenges we face and the successes and goals we accomplish (or not) usually give us cause for reflection. Janet was strongly aware of what she wanted and strongly affected by the emotion of the current

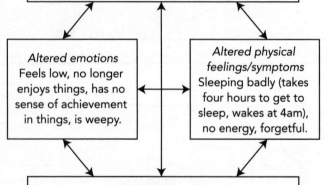

Life situation, relationships and practical problems
Husband has had an affair and left her
three weeks ago.

Altered thinking
'I've been a terrible wife. It's my fault he left.'
'I'll never get another man. My life is over.'
'Everyone will think I've ruined my marriage.'

Altered emotions
Feels low, no longer enjoys things, has no sense of achievement in things, is weepy.

Altered physical feelings/symptoms
Sleeping badly (takes four hours to get to sleep, wakes at 4am), no energy, forgetful.

Altered behaviour
Has stopped getting up early in the morning.
Lies in bed until 11am. Is drinking a bottle of
wine at night to help get to sleep. Has thought
about taking an overdose of paracetamol.
Has stopped answering the phone
to family and friends.

situation. The flow chart illustrates how her emotions have affected her thinking.

The impact has become disabling and negative in part because Janet has been going through the process of reflection which we call 'rumination'. It usually happens as a result of being very aware of the gap between what we would like and what is happening in reality. In her case, she will be reflecting on her unhappiness, the negatives in her present situation, how things might have been, and a wide range of faults, blame and causal factors for the problems she is experiencing. Usually, rumination is accompanied by a reinterpretation of events, and adding negatives to the person's own actions ('he left because *she wasn't good enough*').

The gap between aspiration and current reality can lead to rumination and negative thinking. Imagine for example that you are going to a party but feel tired and out of sorts. As time goes on, you also become conscious of something else: how by going to parties *you should be feeling great* but in fact, are not. Think how you would feel at that point. Many people say they would feel worse than ever.

This is actually a very serious problem because, over a prolonged period of time, rumination diminishes optimism, encouraging negative thinking as the preferred response. Ruminators have trouble getting upsetting thoughts out of their minds; perhaps as a result, they seem to be motivated to avoid unpleasant feelings by trying to rationalize (or 'reason away') anything which seems uncertain or uncontrollable. It is a state of mind which is very self-critical. And being absorbed with what's wrong in a situation, rationalizing things away and being self-critical is a potent recipe. Research links these factors to the tendency among ruminators for procrastination and failure to act promptly in dealing with interpersonal problems.

Perhaps one of the best ways to avoid rumination is maintaining your awareness of the here and now, together with developing an independent, confident and optimistic outlook. These are the characteristics which allow you to take an assertive approach, dealing with problems as they arise rather than leaving them to grow and take on greater significance. A clear sense of purpose helps too. We know that people with strong values are better able to withstand stress and it seems that being purposeful plays a similar role. Controlling the stress reaction, mindfulness and assertiveness limit the power of rumination.

How 'in control' do you feel?

Every day we are faced with situations in which we experience impulses, often triggered by things that we want or desire. This may be an impulse to interfere with how someone is doing a piece of work – thinking we would do it differently or better – or maybe letting rip about how we really feel about something that was done. Alternatively the impulse might be about buying those Louboutin shoes despite the size of your credit card bill. Usually, a lack of control is part of a wider pattern of behaviour, often shown by problems like anger control, difficulty controlling weight or substance abuse.

The ability to control impulses, or more specifically to control the desire to act on them, is primarily about deferred gratification. Being impulsive creates problems in relationships and limits the rational thinking needed to deal with others.

Making emotions manageable

1. Breathe deeply.

2. Take a break, make some coffee, go for a short walk.

3. Use the 'thinking' part of your brain to exert influence on the emotion-creating part.

4. Project into the future – how significant will this situation be next week/month/year?

5. Change the variables – if someone else were involved, would you still feel the same? If it happened at a different time, would it still be so upsetting?

6. Minimize negative automatic thinking – were there no redeeming features at all? Am I speculating about something which may never happen? Am I blaming myself for something I had no control over?

7. Three-minute stress control – try a breathing exercise to reduce the effect of stress.

8. Model a new behaviour – think of someone you value or admire. How would they behave in this situation?

9. Use collaborative language to encourage others to resolve the situation: 'we', 'us', 'together', 'share', etc.

10. Adopt a collaborative approach – what will encourage others to help – being respected? Being helped? Being positive? Being clear? Being valued?

Your emotional intelligence helps you to become aware that behaviour is rarely random. We need to understand what motivates others and how to live or work with them comfortably. If intense emotions, such as stress, frustration or anger are not controlled, inappropriate behaviour can damage relationships.

Controlling outbursts

The first thing you say when you feel angry is usually the worst thing you could say. It takes approximately six seconds from the moment a powerful negative emotion is felt to the time the adrenalin begins to abate. That's about how long you should wait before responding when you're really angry. If you can, simply count to ten; distract yourself.

Controlling impulsive reactions

- Separate the issues involved from the people problems.
- Use distraction and time-outs to keep you cool.
- De-escalate when others get emotional.
- Solve underlying problems by being supportive, analytical and using your listening skills.

Imagine being three or four years old, and being asked to sit in front of a table with your favourite sweet on a plate. If you like, you can eat the sweet straight away. However, if you wait, alone, for fifteen minutes without touching it, you can then have two to eat whenever you like! This was the basis of a research programme at Stanford University. The children responded differently: those who were able to leave the sweet actively found ways to distract themselves, including playing games with their fingers, covering their eyes, singing and talking to themselves. Those who were unable to control themselves did not try distraction: they focused on the object of their desire and ate the sweet within minutes, or in some instances seconds.

Fourteen years later, the children who had been able to resist temptation were more academically successful, socially and emotionally adept, and better able to cope with stress. They pursued challenges rather than giving up when something became difficult; they were seen as independent, confident, trustworthy and prone to showing initiative. And they were all still able to delay gratification for the sake of achieving their goal.

The children who had succumbed to the temptation and had eaten the sweet frequently seemed to be troubled individuals, believing themselves to be 'unworthy', resentful about 'not getting fair shares', and were easily upset by stress. Almost without exception they were less successful in their studies and reports from people they knew suggested they were also prone to distrust and provoking arguments. Fourteen years later they were still unable to delay gratification, or control their impulses.

Being able to control impulses involves emotional intelligence: being aware of the situation you are in, evaluating the possible consequences of simply satisfying your own wishes immediately, and using diversionary tactics to overcome the stress involved in delaying your response.

It is an integral part of Freud's 'reality principle' that achieving your aims *can be made more certain* if you can stave off the urge to satisfy the impulse immediately and behave in a manner that is suitable for the time and place.

A simple example is that, if we were hungry, without the reality principle we might find ourselves simply snatching food from another person's hands and forcing it down without any concern either for the other person's needs or for how we are seen by others.

So diversion is the name of the game. After you've taken a few seconds to allow the stressor hormones from the impulse to dissipate, you can respond in an appropriate way. It may mean leaving something until later when you are more relaxed. You might be more prepared to deal with the issue itself, rather than the emotion caused by the people involved. These two factors need separating; if you feel the need to discuss personal issues, choose a time and place when both of you are relatively calm and can discuss things reasonably. In the heat of the moment it is better to focus on the issue causing concern and try to establish options for dealing with it.

If it's a really heated debate, agree that you take some time out. The chances are everyone is in a calmer frame of mind, more suited to reason. Delays and distractions are a great way to curb impulses so, if you can, try doing something else for a while and plan *exactly* what action you will take. You will take the emotional heat out of the situation and be able to deal with issues in a more rational and constructive manner.

 Do the following statements apply to you? If they do, you are a long way towards being in the collected and analytical state necessary for thinking about the emotions which others are experiencing.

- I am able to control my temper and handle difficulties without them affecting my mood or speech.

- Even when emotional, I can speak in a calm and clear manner.
- I can always calm down quickly when I am very angry.
- When I am very happy I rarely go overboard.
- When dealing with problems, my long-term goals are always the thing which guides my response.
- I can take an independent view of things, even when others disagree.
- I demonstrate optimism, no matter how difficult the situation or other people may be.

Emotional self-control helps you to manage those disruptive emotions which we all feel from time to time – being angry, frustrated, anxious, fearful – but also the excesses we are liable to when feeling good turns into euphoria and 'going over the top'. Euphoric behaviour frequently happens when you feel the need for release – perhaps after a prolonged period of stress or when you experience the relief of something NOT happening.

Emotional self-control enables you to:
- Think clearly and stay focused when others are highly emotional
- Stay composed in difficult moments, giving you the opportunity to stay optimistic and positive
- Keep your impulsiveness under control, or your behaviour when you are feeling anxious or distressed.

Values for working with others

Being able to control yourself in an emotionally intelligent way involves the ability to distance yourself from the situation temporarily, analytical skills to work out how best to accomplish your goals and having a clear sense of purpose. It also involves having positive values for working with others, such as:

Honesty and openness: being true to yourself and your sense of purpose helps others to see you as trustworthy and someone who acts with integrity – even if they don't like what you do. Demonstrating these aspects of self-control means:

- When you are wrong, admitting your mistake and explaining why it may have happened.

- Confronting behaviours and actions in others when they conflict with your beliefs. Being open about why it is a problem and positive about what else might be done in future helps confrontation to become a useful tool for building relationships, rather than a symbol of aggression and need for dominance.

- Being consistent and acting in accordance with your principles is really what ethical behaviour is about. You recognize deeply held beliefs when people act consistently, even when faced with conflicting emotions.

- Reliability and authenticity: doing what you say and being clear it is what you think is right – not creating a perception that you do whatever is expedient.

Adaptability is a good way to demonstrate to others that you are committed to your goals and sense of purpose. Change and uncertainty can be handled more effectively when people believe that they can influence what is happening. It is when change has both negative consequences and involves a loss of control that people become more defensive and less responsive to others trying to influence them.

- Flexibility in handling change means involving others as much as possible and being clear about options, risks and potential opportunities arising from it.

- The multiple demands which are likely to result raise important questions about coping: the time-management involved, clarity of goals, objectives and roles – and above all what the priorities are. If these are handled smoothly, change can become exciting rather than threatening.

- Different 'pairs of spectacles' – how someone sees events needs some thought. Adaptability may involve re-framing the way the situation or people are seen, and taking other perspectives. You need a degree of imagination to see things from others' points of view – more about that when we look at empathy in the next section.

Conscientiousness is a personal value or quality which is seen by others as a marker both of independence and reliability. Human beings have a remarkable ability to rationalize, to find any number of reasons for doing or not doing something. To influence others, the emotionally intelligent person needs to be seen as someone who takes their commitments seriously and models the behaviour they seek from others. This means:

- Meeting your commitments and holding yourself accountable for getting things done

- Keeping promises. Even where this might be a bit inconvenient, it is vital for sustaining trust.

Resilience

Resilience is a very important aspect of emotional self-management. It refers not only to the ability to keep going in adverse or challenging circumstances, but also the ability to think clearly, choosing appropriate and sustainable ways to react whilst dealing with the feelings involved.

The seminal ideas of Carl Jung explore the different preferences we adopt when we perceive information and make judgements about it. Two of the processes we use are critical thinking (analysing, conceptualizing, applying, synthesizing, and/or evaluating information) and the 'affect' or instinctual thinking (emotion, reactions, feelings, values). In the population generally, roughly 50 per cent of people seem to use critical thinking as a preferred way of dealing with life, with a similar number using emotions or affect. These preferences produce very different approaches.

Most people who prefer **critical thinking:**
- are analytical
- use cause-and-effect reasoning
- solve problems with logic
- strive for 'objectivity'
- search for flaws in arguments
- think of equity in terms of decisions.

Most people who value **instinctual or feeling-based judgement:**
- are guided by personal values
- strive for harmony and positive interaction
- search for points of agreement
- want people to be treated as individuals with needs
- use empathy and compassion.

In normal situations, we use both critical and instinctual thinking to some degree, although one tends to dominate. But we need to keep our thoughts and feelings in balance. This means using critical thinking to take active command of not only our thoughts and ideas, but our feelings, emotions, and desires as well. It is critical thinking which provides us with the mental tools needed to take command of what we think, feel, desire, and do.

So resilience involves conscious awareness and the ability to use logical and critical thinking to modify how we feel. Paradoxically, to be emotionally intelligent, we need to ensure that our thinking is not dominated exclusively by emotion.

Emotional intelligence is working on our instincts and thoughts to create a stable and resilient balance for dealing with others.

Willpower

What is willpower? Self-control? Self-discipline? Resolution? Drive? Determination?

We use many different words to describe willpower, a quality or strength which enables you to avoid giving in to things, or keeps you going when circumstances become difficult. A 2003 US study investigated someone's ability to continue trying difficult tasks and testing their persistence in difficult situations. Research psychologist Roy Baumeister used a number of ideas to define willpower more precisely. He suggested that:

- Willpower is demonstrated through the ability to resist short term temptations in order to meet long term goals. We can call this delayed gratification.

- It is shown by the capacity to resist unwanted thoughts, feelings or impulse actions, overriding them with positive, sometimes altruistic intentions.

- Willpower is often characterized by using critical thinking and logical analysis rather than behaviour driven by 'hot' emotional reactions.

- It involves a conscious effort 'by myself, for myself' to both regulate actions and limit them.

- Willpower is limited, and when used up, affects other parts of your life. When exhausted at work, for example, there may be less willpower for social or family activities.

The last point is very important because it suggests that willpower is a limited resource. It can be used up elsewhere, for example managing stress. Researchers tested experimentally whether controlling emotions in difficult circumstances affected the ability of participants to continue with tasks, and found that it had a significantly negative effect. In any given period of time, if willpower is exhausted, we become more vulnerable to other challenges in life, resulting in increased depression, alcohol abuse and impulsive/reactive behaviour.

How can you replenish your store of willpower?

This question is currently the subject of lots of research studies. Many are associated with the idea of mindfulness – being sufficiently self-aware to recognize your current state and being able to relax with other people, to physically and emotionally recuperate, rebuilding your energy. Other studies support sleep, the importance of healthy eating and fructose sugars (like orange juice) having a similar effect. There is also strong evidence about the importance of optimism, psychological well-being and humour for maintaining willpower.

Willpower and well-being are also enhanced by your sense of purpose. It is important therefore that you set goals and targets for yourself, that they are right for you and that you can commit yourself to them.

Choose to pursue goals that are:

- Realistic and achieveable. (Unachievable goals become demotivators.)

- Personally meaningful and congruent with your needs and motives (which enhances commitment).

- Concerned with getting closer to others. (The significance of having a mindset which strongly features helping others is one of the driving forces that enables people to develop their emotional intelligence. Being concerned about others, then taking action to help, seems to be an important feature of psychological well-being.)

- Interesting and absorbing. (Mihaly Csikszentmihalyi wrote an influential book in 1990 about the psychology of optimal experience. In it, he described how a state of 'flow'– what athletes call 'being in the zone', being absorbed and enjoying total focus on something – produces satisfaction, happiness and psychological resilience, all of which are important components for sustaining willpower.)

CASE STUDY

Remember Anthony and Peter? They were two of the pen portraits we looked at in the introduction (pages 1–3).

Anthony spends money like there's no tomorrow and deferred gratification is a concept he finds difficult. He is someone with many serious challenges in his personal life. As result, getting up to go to work each day and coming home to an empty house each night, maintaining the image he likes to project and succeeding in a competitive job pretty well exhausts his stock of willpower. He has become a heavy drinker, is subject to continuous low-level depression. He has no long-term goals to give him focus.

Peter's willpower is also diminished on a daily basis. He struggles to cope with his relationship, having tried, unsuccessfully, to become what his wife wants and tried to ignore his own feelings and hopes. Now, keeping his frustration and anger under control is the biggest act of willpower he has ever faced. It isn't limited to his home life. At work he is seen as volatile and someone to be cautious of and he has to make a supreme effort to maintain relationships with awkward customers. When he gets home, he says he just doesn't want to know. His energy is low and he finds it difficult to make the effort to communicate in a way his wife wants. He has become vulnerable because he is now unable to confront the real causes of his unhappiness.

Being positive about goal-setting

As we have just seen, self-control is more than resisting a dangerous impulse. Real results often come from putting momentary needs on hold in order to pursue more important outcomes. The way we frame our goals and intentions can also make us feel in greater control – making them realistic, achievable and motivating. Being positive is a vital perspective for emotional intelligence. Try to structure your goals with the following questions in mind:

What do you want? (being positive): Goals need to be expressed in positive terms. This isn't about Norman Peale's 'Power of Positive Thinking', nor is it about 'positive' in the sense of being good. It refers to directing your behaviour *towards* something, rather than *away from* something you want to avoid – 'What do I want?' rather than 'What do I not want, or wish to avoid'. Losing weight and stopping smoking are negative outcomes, as are reducing costs and avoiding losing customers. These are worthwhile, but communicate problems and negativity.

Try turning your goals into positive ones by asking 'What behaviour do I want instead?' or 'What results do I need?' For example, if you want to reduce conflict within your team, you can set the goal in terms of identifying opportunities for co-operation or establishing ways of taking into account perspectives from others' roles.

How will you know you are succeeding? (evidence): It's important to know you are on the right track towards your goals and that others who are involved know too. You need adequate feedback, and accurate information which is shared between all who need to know.

Is the goal defined specifically enough? (clarity and focus): Kipling's 'six honest serving men', according to the poem, are 'What and Why and When; and How and Where and Who'. More recent management-speak uses SMART to define clearly what needs to be achieved and so give both you and the others involved more control over what needs to be done. Goals need to be described in ways that are Specific, Measureable, Agreed, Realistic and Timed.

What resources can be devoted to this goal?: Resources tend to fall into five categories (some more relevant than others depending on what you want to achieve). Staying in control and reducing emotional pressure is achieved when your plans reflect realistically the resources available for getting things done. The categories of resources are:

- Objects: equipment, buildings, machinery/technology, books, manuals, etc.

- People: family, friends, colleagues, contacts, stakeholders.

- Role models: anyone you can talk to about their experience of doing similar tasks; someone who understands the problems involved.

- Skills and qualities: personal skills, aptitudes, experience, attitudes, capabilities and values.

- Money and time: Have you got enough, can you obtain more, what are the limitations?

What assumptions do you make? People often make assumptions about what they can achieve based on their interpretation of the situation and the way they predict that the people involved will respond. Emotional intelligence treats beliefs and perspectives as important presuppositions but not immutable laws like gravity or death. We may need to question our own ways of looking at things before we can take action to achieve our goals.

Emotional intelligence treats beliefs as important presuppositions but not facts. They may be an important causal factor for others' (or your own) behaviour but we have a choice about what to believe. Sometimes, despite the obvious problems, we may need to question the mental models that are being applied before we can move towards acting on our goals.

How are beliefs and perceptions connected to reality?

Beliefs are mental models from our experience and history, based on our perceptions. But beliefs also play an important role in the first place by shaping our understanding of what is real. The 'Ladder of Inference' shown overleaf was first put forward by organizational psychologist Chris

Argyris and used by Peter Senge in *The Fifth Discipline: The Art and Practice of the Learning Organization.*

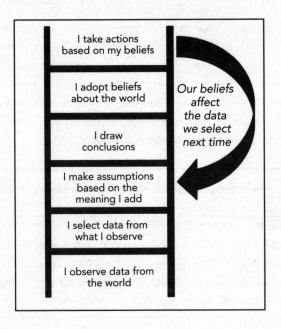

The diagram illustrates the argument that we are selective about the way we experience the world, modifying our real experience by adding meanings, making assumptions and drawing conclusions which both shape and affirm our existing beliefs and future approach. But the beliefs we have adopted create filters, through which we will see and interpret our future experiences. These filters affect which information we will place value on the next time, giving us a picture that may be a long way from what actually happened.

Perhaps the most significant contribution that emotional intelligence can make is to allow our thinking processes to be informed and enriched by our emotions and beliefs – while preserving our ability to see what is happening accurately and without bias.

 Our beliefs and assumptions act as filters for what we see and what we observe.

 How are your goals and beliefs linked?

1. What beliefs do you hold about the following:

- Other people in general?
- Your work colleagues?
- Your boss?
- Improving your career?
- Family and children?
- Having a successful life?

2. What are your short-term and long-term goals? Where do you want to be in five years' time?

3. Which of the beliefs you identified affect your goals?

Assertiveness

For many years, assertiveness has been seen to be a tool of successful people management and leadership. Emotionally intelligent leaders are often seen to be 'comfortable in their own skins' – seeing themselves in an honest but clear light and with good self-esteem. They tend to be straightforward and self-aware – when they are angry they control it but deal with things in a straightforward way, letting others know how they feel. Staying composed when being pressurized, they are able to express themselves with optimism and avoid making themselves the centre when the spotlight should be on the action they want.

Assertiveness is about getting things done and engaging others to help but at the same time acknowledging that others' needs and goals are important. It is about expressing feelings, thoughts, and beliefs in a non-destructive manner which is neither passive nor aggressive. The aim of assertiveness is 'win–win'. It means:

- Expressing views and opinions, wants and needs openly and without fear

- Active listening, to evaluate what response you are getting

- Drawing out the interests and goals of the other person

- Trying to identify common ground whilst being clear about what's important

- Using incentives, problem-solving and encouragement to agree future action.

These behaviours straddle a middle ground between giving in, which involves passively bottling up your emotions and needs, and competing strongly, fighting for your own interests and supremacy. Being assertive rather than dominant makes people more receptive to fitting in with you.

 Assertiveness can be:
- Saying what you think
- Making requests and asking for help
- Negotiating solutions acceptable to everyone
- Refusing requests
- Refusing to be patronized or put down
- Making complaints
- Clarifying expectations
- Expressing your optimism in the face of negativity
- Showing appreciation, affection, hurt feelings, justifiable annoyance
- Overcoming hesitation about 'putting things on the table'
- Giving and receiving compliments
- Working to help others.

Knowing how to express your feelings can help you stay in control of emotions when you feel vulnerable. If you can learn to express yourself in an appropriate way (which doesn't send people running away from you) and at the same time share your thoughts and aspirations, you will be creating a solid foundation upon which everyone knows where they stand.

Increasing your assertiveness

USEFUL TIPS

Here are some tips used in a top-rated UK sales organization where emotional intelligence is considered an essential competency for leadership and management positions:

- Your prime right is to be treated with respect. Equally, we have a responsibility to treat others with similar respect.

- Judge each situation on its merits in terms of fairness, balancing wants with needs, and whilst being self-orientated, your behaviour should not appear selfish.

- Work out what you feel and want, then decide if it is appropriate and fair.

- An assertive person can disagree with you and yet still be your friend; distinguish facts from opinions and people from the issues involved.

- Practise being open about the way your feelings affect you. Acknowledge them if you receive a put-down and say in a clear and firm manner that the person's comment or behaviour is unacceptable to you.

- When you need to be assertive with others, ask for more information. Hidden in their remarks can be assumptions you can spotlight.

- If someone is angry, find out what is behind it. There may be a more constructive form of discussion to be had.

- Be polite when you disagree with someone. Tell them your preferences using clear and simple statements.

- Be prepared to repeat what you have said as many times as necessary until others show they have heard and understood the point you are making.

---

3. Understanding others

Looking outwards, understanding other people

If you have read the preceding sections, you know that an important part of emotional intelligence is about tuning in to your own feelings. Now we need to tune into others' emotions and their needs too. Understanding other people involves first deciding to switch your attention away from yourself. You need information about feelings and emotions, and to get it you need to use effective listening skills. You need to recognize emotional cues; show empathy; analyze why people behave in the way they do, understanding the effect that their situation can have on people; and in particular show that you are responding to their needs and concerns.

For some people there is a basic problem with this, and it goes to the heart of what emotional intelligence is about. *Should we care about or be interested in other people?* The cultures in many communities and organizations still push people towards self-interest. In these settings, you need to prove that you are better than anyone else. You do it by celebrating others' weakness. Not only does your company, for example, have *external* competitors, competition between individuals and groupings *inside* the organization is rife.

Though it appeals to the more competitive part of us, self-interest doesn't really work in the long term. If you don't listen to others, or simply don't care (particularly if you show it), can you really expect support, commitment or ideas from others to help you in the future? Many organizations have worked hard on emotional intelligence to eliminate internal competition, to eliminate barriers and to eliminate the behaviours which create them. Emotional intelligence has become a sought-after competence precisely because it fosters awareness of others' needs; using it develops better relationships.

Being overly competitive and trying to dominate others creates problems when you try to achieve your goals. Most people resent being dominated and may respond using subtle (or not so subtle) ways of avoiding future contact. When relationships are difficult or you need to obtain co-operation – perhaps getting repeat orders or confronting difficulties, you need to understand exactly *why* people take the view they do. People with low emotional intelligence will often focus on the issue involved and will get what *they* see as the right answer, but without paying heed to the perspectives others take, their interpretation of events or the needs they have.

Another problem is that the more dominating you appear, the less information you are likely to get. Making the effort to understand others, using your listening and critical thinking skills, helps you distinguish symptoms from causes, evaluate risk and potential, identify levers and opportunities, and identify where you can take appropriate action. In the real world, there are few dividing lines between what people think, say and feel – these things are all interrelated, and they are all involved in every aspect of human behaviour. All of which creates a complicated picture when we deal with other individuals, and even more so when dealing with teams or groups. Emotional intelligence and social awareness is about gathering data – data equally as important as information about costs and margins, product performance or error rates. Social awareness produces valuable information for making decisions and taking action.

Using empathy

I spoke recently to a nurse who had just retired. 'We always needed to help our patients feel supported and that at least *we* understood what they were going through,' she said. 'It was difficult sometimes because when they were upset I often felt teary too.' In the same conversation, another nurse, one working with cancer patients, said, 'I know. Poor things, I often feel sorry for them.' A considerate and kind thing to feel and characteristic of many nurses, but what this comment shows isn't empathy. It is sympathy.

Sympathy is an important building block for good relationships and is something we do when others experience difficult or even tragic situations – redundancy, injury or bereavement for example. In this type of situation, people feel comforted when others express how they feel about them. But it has a different function to empathy:

Sympathy stems from judgement of someone's situation and is a reflection of how *you* feel. It is caring and helpful, but it is about you. And it may not employ many critical, analytical skills.

Empathy is about the other person's perspective and feelings. Showing you understand enables you to get closer and gain trust. Most emotionally intelligent people draw on empathy as a tool for relationship-building and understanding problems. It is based on effective listening, communication and critical analysis.

Empathy is characterized by several elements:

1. Recognizing that the other person is experiencing significant feelings (which might be positive or negative) and some sense of why that is happening.

2. Saying something which demonstrates both that you understand what they are going through and why. This is normally a combination of:
   - a reflective statement like 'You must feel …'
   - a reason, e.g. some shared experience ('I had a similar …')
   - affirmation ('… which made me feel pretty low too').

3. Offering a next step which might help and at the same time, enhance your relationship ('Have you thought how you might …?' or 'Would it be of any help if …?').

This type of contact with people can be the beginning of further communication and a deepening of the quality of the relationship. It implies that you are concerned about the other person. It shows that concern in a practical way and demonstrates your preparedness to help.

Behaving in this way requires you to do something that isn't always easy – suspending your own judgement and putting your own interests on the back burner for a while. Research conducted in the US suggests that your factual knowledge about the people you are with is not enough to ensure you will be good at empathizing. To understand what they are experiencing you need to understand the experience and values they draw on. Knowing how *they* look at things from the *inside*, rather than relying on *your outside perspective*, is the key.

 Empathy is neither good nor bad, nor is it dependent on how much of a people person you are. It is a neurological process; the ability to visualize emotions in other people is a survival tool which, because we are social animals, is hard-wired into the way all our brains work. You just have to activate it.

To understand the process that takes place, let's take an example about one emotion that has been the subject of a great deal of research: disgust.

THINK ABOUT IT

In a café, because I am engrossed in reading a particular article, I pick up an old cup from the table without thinking. I am about to drink when I realize the cup is cold, then see that it is covered in lipstick and other stains and has a cigarette butt in the bottom. I react by turning away from the smell and sight of the cup, place it away from me, wrinkle my nose, grimace and say, 'Oh, for goodness sake, that's disgusting!'

Reading the above, what tells you, specifically, that what I am feeling in this situation is disgust? Is it something I said, or was there more? How do you know what my disgust actually feels like?

If we see someone else picking up a cup and reacting to its contents, a chain of mechanisms in the brain registers and processes information and emotions. Physical actions and movement by others are handled differently to the way our understanding of their intentions and emotions are processed. The brain does this by differentiating between types of actions we observe:

- **Cold actions** – those actions devoid of emotional content, such as movement (when we see someone pick up the cup) – are processed in the 'thinking and deciding part' of the brain, the parieto-frontal cortex, as neutral data. This results in us knowing what is physically happening.

- **Warm actions** – data regarding the person's intentions (in this case, say, picking up the cup to throw it away, or to throw it at us) – involves our powers of imagination. So-called mirror neurons activate a representation or memory of what someone's intentions *might* be. Our frontal cortex then decides if the imaginary representation is relevant. This is an important survival skill based on instinct and experience, and because intention relates to some future action, the level of emotional processing in the brain is low.

- **Hot actions** are when the brain is processing emotions and threats, like when some hazard is present or, in our example, the disgust felt at the content of the cup. Using signals like facial expressions, voice tones, speech and gestures, the same mirror neurons create a representation in *you* of what may be being felt by the person holding the cup. But instead of linking to the cortex to understand it, the brain uses areas which are much more involved with creating emotional reactions in your body (the amygdala) and a place in the older, mammalian brain known as the insula. This part of the brain is concerned with survival and safety and is sensitive to threats like rancid food and poisoned water. These two areas create intense images, drawing on *your* real emotions. It may seem as though you are experiencing the same emotion that you would if you were in the situation yourself.

Developing empathy will enable you use your emotional intelligence much more effectively than consciously trying to work it out. Reading non-verbal clues and voice tones will help you understand when people are feeling low. Use your imagination to speculate why they might feel that way. It's not difficult; your brain is hard-wired to do it.

For something like 25 years, the topic of inferring others' thoughts and feelings has been addressed by a field of research called 'empathetic accuracy'. Normally developing children have the capacity to infer **action** and **intention** by the age of four or five. But the ability to identify others' **emotional states** takes longer, often not developing until adolescence. This ability may play an important role in teenagers' social development and the final hard-wiring of the brain seems to happen towards the end of adolescence.

Other research tells us that being able to judge others' feelings accurately are characteristics which go along with abstract critical thinking, non-dogmatic personalities, feelings of self-worth and well-being, together with an appreciation of aesthetics (form and regularity). Both good and poor judges seem to be anxious or neurotic to a similar degree.

Empathy involves reading the behaviours and actions of others, understanding the intensity of the feelings involved and choosing the most appropriate behaviour to engage them positively.

Knowing when to respond to others involves reading others' non-verbal communication, voice tones and actions. We look for gestures, body posture, eye contact, vocal tones and general behaviour.

Focus and roles

Anthropologists looking at new island communities have found that groups respond to people with high emotional intelligence because the people begin to form bonds and alliances based on things they have in common or things they do or do not agree on. People who talk about others – their situations, concerns or achievements – are most highly valued. Most importantly, they build relationships and begin to care for and trust each other. Regardless of your work ethic, once you begin to know someone and respect them, you will support them, you won't betray them and you won't 'vote them off the island'. The one we are most willing to 'vote off' is the one we don't know much about.

The basis of interpersonal influence is not simply the power of your personality or fluency. It lies in the strength of the relationships and social bonds which exist, whether in a team, organization or community. Those relationships stem from what you are doing and how you communicate during the time you spend together. Much of that is defined by your role, and how much emphasis you place on task or people in your conversation.

In the island research, tension and frustration developed between those people who communicated solely about the tasks they had to do and the few individuals who had needs and relationships as their sole focus. The other more emotionally intelligent members practised both task and socio-emotional actions equally; the social contact became the glue which enabled people to get on with their jobs, whilst feeling positive and supporting each other. If we are ONLY engaged in task-oriented actions, we might as well be pieces of machinery – easily ignored with no regrets or feelings of remorse.

Someone who behaves in a confident way, is concerned about the needs of others, listens well and has ideas is likely to increase social cohesion in any group of people, with many benefits. Simply being concerned with what *you* are doing, alone, is ineffective.

REMEMBER THIS!!! Confident behaviour stemming from both a sense of purpose and valuing relationships is important. EI is about developing relationships; what you do in the relationship is equally important. Your vision and your goals, openness, getting things done, and being concerned about others gets you valued.

Being receptive to others

Good communication is the foundation of emotionally intelligent relationships, both personally and professionally. But we communicate with much more than words. Research shows that the majority of the messages we send are nonverbal. Nonverbal communication includes our facial expressions, gestures, eye contact, posture and, even more significantly, our tone of voice.

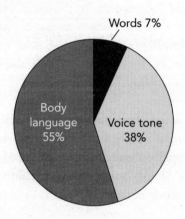

Three elements of communication

What are nonverbal communication and body language?

Nonverbal communication is a natural, unconscious language that broadcasts our true feelings and intentions in any given moment, and clues us in to the feelings and intentions of those around us.

When we interact with others, we continuously give and receive wordless signals. All of our nonverbal behaviours – the expression on our faces, the gestures we make, the way we sit, how fast or how loud we talk, how close we stand, how much eye contact we make – send strong messages. These messages don't stop when you stop speaking either. Even when you're silent, you're still communicating nonverbally.

You listen with both your ears and your eyes; nonverbal communication is a channel for information about primary feelings and attitudes.

The way you listen, look, move and react tells the other person whether or not you care, if you're being truthful and how well you're listening. When your nonverbal signals match up with the words you're saying, they increase trust, clarity and rapport. When they don't, they generate tension, mistrust and confusion.

What we say and what we communicate through body language are two totally different things. When faced with these mixed signals, the listener has to choose whether to believe your verbal or nonverbal message, and, in most cases, they're going to choose nonverbal.

Psychologist and renowned expert in human communication Albert Mehrabian identified three aspects of this information channel which provide the cues for interpreting behaviour.

- We move toward people and things we like and avoid or move away from those we dislike. **Immediacy cues** (including eye contact, touching, leaning forward and smiling) communicate positive feelings, liking and pleasure.

- When we are interested in communicating with someone else, we tend to be more animated. **Arousal cues** (including varied vocal tone, animated facial expressions and movement in general) show levels of commitment.

- Beliefs about relative or perceived status, position, importance and power are communicated by **dominance cues**. (For instance, a person of high status will tend to have a relaxed body posture when interacting with a person of lower status.)

One reason why these cues are important is because it is difficult to control them all at once – with the result that it is difficult to portray something that isn't true. It comprises a channel of highly reliable information which research suggests can be as much as 70 per cent of the messages we understand from other people. And there is also evidence that it is the most important, deeply held issues which trigger nonverbal communication of real feelings.

Pick up on the following cues to demonstrate empathy and emotional intelligence:

- Facial expressions
- Body movements and posture
- Gestures
- Eye contact
- Touch
- Space
- Voice

 Emotionally intelligent people use nonverbal communication for:

- Reinforcement: they can make the message the person is making verbally more powerful.

- Contradiction: they can contradict messages other individuals are trying to convey – closing down communication when necessary to prevent disagreement from getting out of hand.

- Substitution: they can substitute for a verbal message. For example, a person's eyes can often convey a far more vivid message than words.

- Complementing: they may add to or complement a verbal message. A boss who pats a person on the back in addition to giving praise can increase the impact of the message whilst adding a further dimension, such as personal warmth.

- Accenting: they can underline all or part of a verbal message. Touching the table, for example, can underline a key part of the message or indeed the whole thing. But it can easily communicate frustration or impatience too. Watch out for the signals you are sending.

Political sensitivity and power

All human interaction involves power and influence. Many people are unaware of the influence they exert on others, and many are equally unaware of how necessary and constructive power and influence can be in creating collaborative relationships and building effective groups. The skills emotional intelligence brings to this aspect of life are in understanding the way power, and the use of it, influences people. This leads to the ability to focus on achievement of personal and organizational goals despite the negative impact of interpersonal politics.

One of the most fascinating aspects of people with high levels of emotional intelligence is their ability to accomplish complex tasks by drawing on their understanding of the dynamics of their organizations – which buttons you press to get results, who has influence and how they can be persuaded to use it.

A political environment can be defined as a place in which the person doing something is more significant than what is being done. If some people make a proposal, it gets taken up. If others do so, it is viewed sceptically. They are places in which winning and losing are important and power bases concentrate influence. Some people say that 'so long as there are organizations, there will be politics' (with a small p). Although they may decry politics, they do little to create any change. People who play political games are often self-interested, rather than concerned with the needs of others (or, for that matter, the organization itself). They assume others are like them.

To play, however, they must read the emotional 'temperature' of situations, know what motivates others and have sufficient empathy to anticipate how people may respond if particular events take place. Emotional intelligence in organizations utilizes those skills but recognizes that most people want to be part of something. It may be a group, team or community but as social animals there is a wealth of research pointing to the need for a sense of belonging.

This provides opportunities for emotionally intelligent leaders to engage with staff, building a real sense of purpose which creates communities of interest, motivation and more effective performance. Other, less emotionally intelligent, leaders will fail to take into account the views of their staff, foisting a unilateral vision on them and pretending it is shared. The result is a failure to tap into the energy created by emotional intelligence.

Have a vision for your life: If you want to create impact with other people, you need to have a vision or sense of purpose that can motivate you and help you to achieve what you consider to be important. It is likely to be about the values you hold but it also needs to be practical. Set goals and aim for appropriate rewards. Probably more importantly, develop a plan, set out a strategy for getting there and keep to your plan.

Fuel your passion: Motivation is largely emotional. What could you find yourself passionate about doing?

Work hard enough to get results: Results enhance motivation by showing what you can achieve. Hard work implies results and the better results you get, the more your motivation will grow. Motivation and results interact!

Take time for mindfulness and give your feelings a name when you become conscious of them.

Put positive thoughts into your mind: Read, listen to advice and learn more about your motivation and what drives you.

Ride the momentum when it comes: Sometimes things go well and sometimes they don't. That is normal. Make sure you feel good about yourself when things go the way you want them to go.

Highly charged emotional situations

Upset people often have:

- Low levels of logic and highly emotional perspectives
- Little knowledge of reality (i.e. how the system works) and unrealistic expectations
- Deeper problems than may be apparent on first sight
- Previous bad experiences gearing them for confrontation or emotional instability
- Anxiety, frustration and anger.

Your emotional intelligence can keep relationships at a functional, cooperative level if you manage the occasional (or in some cases, regular) outbursts of emotion that occur when people are angry, frustrated, anxious, or feel put down or snubbed. Perhaps strangely, the process which leads to such an outburst usually begins some time before the event or situation which triggers it.

Trigger events, like the computer going wrong *again* or unthinking criticism, are events that trigger *a breakdown in control* – and usually result from accumulated frustration. There are usually precedents for the trigger and you need to know others well enough to anticipate what 'pushes their buttons'.

Triggers are usually followed by increasingly heightened emotional states as the limbic system triggers the body's 'fight or flight' hormonal reaction (which we discussed in the context of stress management – see pages 66–68). The peak of that upward curve is sometimes described as the 'crisis' – the expression of anger, the tears, the slamming of doors and particularly with young adolescents the self-inflicted or targeted violence. When a person's 'fight or flight' reaction has been triggered and they are at, or approaching, the 'crisis', there are various things we can do to help.

Being aware of pressures before they get out of hand is important. Being sensitive to others' frustrations and helping to maintain calm through quietly supportive action is essential. Recognizing that outbursts can lead to destructive behaviour and words to be regretted afterwards requires sensitivity to what is causing the outburst and quiet de-escalating action during and after the crisis. But crucially, the emotionally intelligent approach recognizes that when the precedents for emotional outbursts are not dealt with, they will create problems repeatedly. Your EI helps you to create a relationship where you can find a long-term solution to the underlying issues involved. Empathy and listening skills are essential.

The graph opposite shows how the body reacts when something triggers an emotional response. The terms below the curve describe the various stages, while the terms above the curve describe what you can do at each stage to help a person who is going through this.

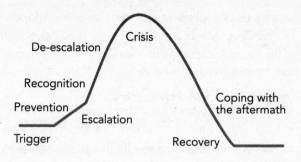

Crisis

De-escalation

Recognition

Coping with the aftermath

Prevention

Escalation

Trigger

Recovery

De-escalating highly emotional situations

Here are some de-escalation techniques used by experienced mental health nurses in a crisis:

- Assess the situation promptly. If you see signs and symptoms of a person entering into crisis, intervene early.

- Maintain a calm demeanour and voice.

- Use problem-solving with the individual – ask 'What will help now?'

- Use empathy: try to understand things from their point of view and what they are feeling.

- Reassure the individual where possible.

- Find a quieter place to talk if possible.

- Offer to help.

- Engage the individual, trying to get them to talk about mechanical or practical things around them.

- Don't crowd the individual; give him or her space.

- Be aware of yourself – your look, your tone.

- Use open-ended questions.

- Give the individual time to think.

- Ignore challenges; redirect challenging questions.

- Allow venting of strong feelings – encourage them to express their feelings.

- Pace your response – don't try to rush things.

- Don't say 'you must …'. Explain why a particular action is needed.

- Avoid power struggles.

- Set limits and tell them what the expectation is and why.

- Be careful with your nonverbal behaviours – what do they communicate?

- Be aware of the individual's nonverbal behaviours.

- Be clear – use simple language.

- Language: follow the rule of five (no more than five words in a sentence, five letters in a word, e.g. 'Would you like a chair?')

- Use reflective technique – 'So are you saying that …?'

- Be prepared to agree to disagree.

Interim questionnaire

We have covered a lot of ground in the three major components of emotional intelligence discussed so far. The fourth EI skill set (covered in the next chapter) is not something you can learn about alone. It covers relationships with people you know. Their reaction to you is something you need to understand before making the best of the tools and tips which are covered. So, ask someone you trust (who will be honest and who knows you well) to give you their assessment of you, based on the following statements.

For simplicity, use a 1–5 scale, where 1 is low and 5 is high. There may be some that they will not feel they can answer and if so, you will need to give yourself a rating instead. Add the scores and write in the sub-totals for each section. There is no total score.

There are also two general questions at the end. Get feedback on these from a different appraiser.

Your self-awareness: Your ability to see yourself and to understand your impact on the world you live in. Emotionally intelligent behaviours include:
- Can tell when own mood is changing
- Can tell when own emotions are affecting performance
- Quickly realizes when starting to lose temper
- Quickly realizes when thoughts are turning negative

- Reflects and learns from experience
- Is open to feedback
- Is able to show a sense of humour and laugh at themselves
- Shows confidence in own capabilities
- Is guided by internal belief and value system
- Is able to articulate feelings and emotions appropriately.

Managing your emotions: The ability to control unproductive behaviours, manage feelings, impulses and energy. Emotionally intelligent behaviours include:
- Is prepared to admit own mistakes
- Acts ethically and can stand scrutiny
- Will take a tough, principled stand even if it is unpopular
- Challenges unethical actions in others
- Just gets on with things when angry
- Engages in self-talk to manage feelings of anger or anxiety
- Able to concentrate when feeling anxious
- Thinks clearly and stays focused under pressure
- Remains cool in the face of others' anger or aggression
- Stays composed, positive and unruffled even in trying moments.

Self-motivation: Your ability to pursue goals with commitment, passion, energy and emotion. Emotionally intelligent behaviours include:
- Is driven to meet objectives and standards
- Sets challenging goals

- Constantly strives to improve performance
- Is ready to seize opportunities
- Mobilizes others through own efforts
- Is motivated by hope of success rather than fear of failure
- Bounces back quickly after a setback
- Kick-starts self into action when needed
- Willingly changes the way of doing things when current methods are not working
- Able to lift energy level to tackle and complete boring tasks.

Managing your relationships: The ability to manage and build networks of relationships. Emotionally intelligent behaviours include:
- Actively seeks ways of resolving conflict
- Is skilled at winning people over
- Demonstrates empathy with others' feelings
- Enables others to trust and confide in them
- Respects and relates well to others from varying backgrounds
- Challenges bias and intolerance
- Accurately reads key power relationships
- Understands the forces that shape others' views
- Uses a win–win approach
- Fosters open communication.

Emotion coaching: Your ability to help others develop their emotional capabilities both by direct intervention and example. Emotionally intelligent behaviours include:

- Raises morale of others and makes them feel good
- Encourages enthusiasm in others
- Paints a positive picture of the future that others buy into
- Senses others' emotions and responds accordingly
- Communicates own feelings to others
- Leads by example; is a role model
- Builds rapport with others
- Makes and maintains personal friendships with work colleagues
- Models respect, helpfulness, honesty and co-operation.

Scoring

Add your scores for each section and multiply by four to give you a percentage score. It should give you a guide about how the person giving you feedback saw your level of EI, using the model of emotional intelligence in this book. Think about whether it surprises you and whether you agree or disagree. Use your scores to point you towards further reading about any areas where you did less well than you expected.

Finally

Find someone else you know to give you a different view about how well you relate to others. Ask them these questions (they don't need to give a score):

- What values do they believe you hold, as a result of their contacts with you?
- How easy is it for other people to be really open with you?

4. Managing your relationships

In work and in our personal lives, relationships take many forms. It may be a close partnership or marriage, a business relationship with a client or colleague or any of the less close relationships we form with the networks of people in our address books and email inboxes. Emotionally intelligent people are usually more satisfied with relationships (including their social and personal ones) and perhaps because they work at maintaining them, they are usually happier and more positive about contacts with other people.

Every day we need to communicate in some way with other people, some of them well known to us, others more distant. How we get on with them depends on many things: how we communicate, the type of people they are, what values we each hold, the histories we have experienced together – the list goes on.

The skills of emotional intelligence that you use to maintain and nurture relationships are central to your success. For best effect, you need to make a conscious effort to put a number of key building blocks in place:

Building blocks for managing relationships:

- Show people that you value them.

- Seek mutual understanding and information sharing.

- Fine-tune your presentation to appeal to the listeners' needs.

- Build consensus and support wherever possible.

- Communicate with clear and convincing messages.

- Use negotiation rather than dominance.

- Be upfront and straightforward, avoiding games or office politics.

- Analyse performance and root causes of problems.

- Approach conflict constructively, staying aware of others' feelings.

- Bring disagreements into the open, and help de-escalate them.

- Be tactful when responding to others.

- Orchestrate win–win solutions.

- Understand uncertainty and metanoia (see pages 147–150).

Relationships can range from being mere acquaintances to meaningful friendships that last for years. Building them isn't new. You will have been using your emotional intelligence to build relationships during your entire life. They begin with predictions about the likelihood that you can 'connect' with other people based on a number of different types of information.

You use three levels of information to make predictions:

Cultural information: General characteristics you share with a large number of people, such as the area you live in, language habits, gender norms.

Social information: Information about membership in a group, such as 'pensioner', 'singer', 'martial artist', 'salesperson'. Stereotyping is also relevant here – the assumptions that you apply to someone based on conventional patterns of background, appearance, speech, accent.

Personal information: The special or unique characteristics of that particular person.

Stages of relationships

Below are set out the different stages of relationships, showing how shared information progressively makes a relationship stronger:

First meeting: All relationships start here.
- Cultural and sociological information is shared.
- Superficial discussions take place, creating a 'ritualistic' relationship.
- No real self-disclosure.

Friendly relationship: This is the stage that most relationships exist in – people you know but are not real friends.
- No real commitment.

- Opinions and feelings shared are not very personal.
- More likely to be accurate in interpreting nonverbal cues; reactions less stereotyped.

Involved relationship:
- Becoming closer involves the self-disclosure of personal information and feelings.
- Talking about feelings becomes easier; individual-level information is shared.
- Real interpersonal communication begins to happen at this stage.
- Empathizing is focused on deeper emotions.

Stable relationship:
- Each person knows the other well on an individual level.
- You don't use stereotypes to interpret each other's behaviours.
- You are likely to disclose your viewpoint or personal matters openly.
- Maintaining relationships at this stage requires great time and effort.

Relationships can move forward and backward through these stages. As they move forward, the growth of trust and openness takes place, increasing openness and depth of communication. Sometimes relationships get into trouble, with break-ups, personal arguments and, very often, simply drifting apart because of lack of maintenance. A major cause of difficulty is when issues of power need to be resolved – who takes the lead, who has freedom to act, whose viewpoint matters and so on.

Here are some key ways you can develop and maintain relationships.

Confirming your view that the other person is important. This might involve:

- Recognition of their existence by simply looking at and listening to them
- Greetings, recognition, responses
- Expressing and interpreting feelings.

Self-disclosure: Voluntarily sharing personal information or feelings with another person for the purpose of building a relationship. This can be planned or spontaneous, but there must be trust in the relationship. It involves risk – everyone needs to judge the level of trust before making disclosures.

Empathizing. This will involve:

- Becoming aware of subjects people feel emotionally about
- Learning to determine another's feelings or background
- Learning to put yourself in another's place.

Giving feedback about your thoughts and reactions. This gives the other person information about your position and feelings and helps them keep their own behaviour on track. It should follow these principles:

- Separate the issue from the people.
- Talk in terms that describe, not judge.

- Talk in terms of the present situation.
- Understand what nonverbal message you are communicating.
- Use 'I' messages to describe your thoughts and feelings assertively.

Being open-minded. This might involve:
- The ability to be flexible when reacting to situations or people
- Avoiding the belief that there is only one way to solve problems
- Changing a point of view
- Looking for new ideas and experiences.

Choosing appropriate language. For instance:
- First names indicate closeness. Using them before the relationship has been established might signal disrespect, particularly with older people.
- Choice of words can indicate feelings. For example, saying 'That's stupid' implies that you feel they are stupid. (You can also listen to how others express their feelings through their choice of words – words like 'uncomfortable' or 'hellish' are very expressive and give a good indication of how positively or negatively a person feels.)

Monitoring others' nonverbal communication. This involves:
- Observing facial expressions, eye contact, gestures and posture

- Noticing vocal characteristics such as tone of voice
- Noticing silences and being aware of whether they are comfortable silences or negative silences.

Language – a positive approach

One of the most emotionally intelligent individuals I know is unrelentingly positive. His view of the world is that it is full of possibilities and that the only thing preventing us from achieving them is our constraining mindsets. We often tend to be problem-focused, risk-aware, depressed by difficulty and conscious of how many things are wrong. Many of us live our lives mainly being aware of what is wrong. Cognitive scientists exploring constructs (ways of looking at the world) have found that seeing negatives is very characteristic of people with high construct ranges. To put it another way, brighter people tend to see weaknesses more easily, and focus on them.

My friend's view is that whilst we may face lots of difficulties, it is more important to create a sense of energy and possibility within ourselves and among the people we relate to. His recipe for how to do that is based on using positive language, humour and smiling. He also gave me a good tip about why the language we use is sometimes self-defeating:

Remember that taking action requires a chain of *positive* instructions (thoughts) leading to changes in behaviour. So when someone gives us a *negative* message, we need to change it to enable us to act.

For example, someone says to us, 'Don't eat cakes!' The unconscious message we absorb is a positive – the original statement minus the 'Don't'. We turn the active part of the message into 'eat cakes'.

So, at every opportunity, even though we know we shouldn't eat them, we look at them, think about them and salivate over them. The 'Don't' makes life difficult.

Similarly, we could say to someone, 'Don't feel bad' or 'Don't worry', but if they don't absorb the 'Don't', then the message only serves to make them aware of feeling bad, or of the things they might worry about. We can unwittingly programme ourselves and others to fail in our objectives.

An optimistic and positive attitude is an essential tool for emotional intelligence. My friend suggests making more use of positive speech in which we turn '**don't** do' into a '**can** do' at every opportunity.

For example:

'Don't feel bad' becomes 'We should all feel good'.

'You may have a problem' becomes 'We can handle any problems this way …'.

Increasing your influence by being authentic

Whether we like it or not, we all carry labels which say what kind of people we are. They may be attached by us, saying, 'this is who I am' and 'this is how I want others to see me'. We resolve, for example, the anxiety that going into an unknown situation poses by presenting ourselves in particular ways. Maybe we want to be seen as dynamic or reflective, in charge or at others' disposal; perhaps the consummate professional or the go-getter for whom rules aren't important.

Or these labels may be attached by others – 'cheerful' for example, or 'cautious', 'friendly' and so on. One of the difficulties that results from this labelling is that others then expect us to live up to our labels – the ones which they've stuck on us – and their labels are used to judge the way we act.

Labels are often shorthand descriptions of how we perceive people, but they have an important flaw: they rarely tell the whole truth. Cautious people sometimes take huge risks when personal emotions are in play; go-getters can often be slowed down when they don't feel valued; friendly people frequently suffer confidence problems when they feel rejected.

 What labels do you attach to others in the relationships you think of as important? Do people attach any particular labels to you?

Authenticity is the permission we give ourselves to be who we really are, warts and all. It frees us to communicate openly without concerns about not being recognized, understood, accepted for who we are, or being invisible or overshadowed by others. Labelling is an inevitable shorthand we use to categorize people; emotional intelligence, however, goes beyond such stereotypes, and enables us to build relationships which are honest and forthright. Good relationships need trust, an absence of fears and a warts-and-all recognition of who we are. The building blocks for managing relationships as described in the preceding section show that emotionally intelligent individuals not only say that they value people, but show it in their dealings with others. Relationships prosper when we allow ourselves to be open, authentic and genuine.

Being authentic, owning your beliefs and demonstrating them in your interactions is one of the features of what is often called 'charisma'. Professor Richard Wiseman led a study in 2005 which suggests that charisma is 50 per cent innate and 50 per cent trained. His tips include keeping an open body posture and communicating your ideas clearly and with commitment.

Individuals who have this characteristic are people with the ability to monitor emotions within themselves and others, using it to communicate a compelling vision that draws commitment in a shared direction. It is a style of communication that engages with people; it involves being prepared to both give and receive information, and it is informal rather than relying on formality or status. It uses words like trust, loyalty, devotion, commitment, inspiration, admiration, outstanding, exceptional. A recent overview of the effectiveness of this approach identified it as the ability of a person to get an intense moral commitment and a strong identification from colleagues and others.

Charismatic people let others know that they matter, and that being around them is enjoyable. Behaviours demonstrated by charismatic people include genuine smiles, nodding when others talk, perhaps briefly touching someone on the upper arm if appropriate, and maintaining eye contact. In groups, they move around to appear enthusiastic, lean slightly forward and look at everyone involved.

They achieve influence by being clear, fluent, forceful and articulate, evoking imagery and using an upbeat tempo (slowing occasionally to create tension or add emphasis). Influence distinguishes high performers from others. People with this ability are skilled at winning people over and fine-tune their contributions so that they appeal to the interests or needs of other people, building support for ideas and projects and developing 'coalitions of interest'. They have an unerring sense of which button to press and what will convince someone to share their ideas. Technically skilled people become relatively ineffective when they can't communicate their ideas in ways that convince others.

Authentic people have increased influence when their ideas move beyond the status quo and make a difference. They are prepared to be controversial, counterintuitive and innovative, but also work at being simple to understand.

In ambiguous or uncertain situations, people look to the behaviour of authentic, confident and consistent others for a template to help them cope. Emotionally intelligent group members who can articulate vision, passion and commitment are invested with social leadership in their groups, irrespective of their formal roles. Other behaviours they show are a balanced approach to risk-taking, standing up for beliefs, promoting the team and acting for others when help is needed.

These behaviours also give an opportunity to communicate other messages, for example, showing others that you value them and that their contribution is important; maybe also communicating your own positive outlook, despite the problems and stresses the team may feel.

Emotionally intelligent communication is not just about being clear and concise. It incorporates charismatic behaviours to create impact.

Emotional intelligence in personal relationships

The American poet and humorist Ogden Nash wrote that the art of keeping a relationship alive comes down to being able to say you are sorry and avoiding getting your own back – rubbing it in when your partner gets it wrong. Most people recognize that actually this takes quite a bit of work, involving empathy, self-control and a practical understanding of human needs and feelings. Nash's succinct idea is a good, practical guide and broadly supported by marital and relationships studies – with one or two interesting subtleties.

Researchers have found that people in strong relationships see their partners in a very positive light – some might say through 'rose-tinted spectacles'. This leads to glossing over their faults or simply not noticing them. Their expectations, attributing charitable intentions to each other in the face of less-than-exemplary behaviour, are equally important. Expecting the best, leading to noticing what is good, is about faith and the self-fulfilling prophecy. Expectations of a successful relationship lead to many things – subtle behaviours which imply valuing the other person, belief in their ability, liking time together and so on. Recent long-term studies suggest that optimistic expectations also cause small changes in communication skills, particularly openness, listening, reinforcement (e.g. nodding, saying 'okay' to show agreement) and smiling.

At the same time, you don't create positive feelings simply in the absence of negative ones; being neutral (or having a 'stiff upper lip') leads to an emotional disconnection rather than positive regard. The EI skills of empathy, emotional awareness and feelings management are important in generating positive feelings and mutual regard.

Positive feelings are generated when people in any relationship display openness, agreeableness, self-control and active management of their own feelings. It is not passive nor is it neutral. You have to work at it.

Ultimately, the thing that best defines an emotionally intelligent relationship – whether personal or work-based – is the ability to generate a 'climate of appreciation and value'. This helps meet the need we have for each other's approval and for being valued as individuals. People who feel this way are more likely to withstand the 'ups and downs' of life, the inevitable disappointments and periodic problems that occur in every relationship. Even in the most well-established relationships, partners still want each other's admiration and approval and to feel cherished by their significant other.

In the interests of balance, however, remember that whilst emotional intelligence increases the chances of maintaining a successful, long-term relationship, it cannot on its own guarantee it. In a marriage, the partners must want to be together and be committed to making it work. In a team, there must be reasons for the members to need to work together rather than achieve on their own. People in a relationship must take responsibility for each others' needs and show compassion, looking out for problems which might affect them and being prepared to help.

The emotionally intelligent relationship must have purpose and maintenance, and provide added value for both people.

Identifying feelings

Marriage and our close personal relationships are the source of some of our deepest emotions and the extent to which couples can understand, communicate and manage them plays a crucial role in their happiness. Much of the research into emotionally intelligent marriages (and partnerships) has focused on the people's capacity to identify emotions in themselves and each other (see below) but much less on the skills associated with communication, management and expression. It seems that individuals vary considerably in their ability to clearly describe their feelings. It also seems that habitual expression of ambiguous or confusing signals of emotion (like someone both smiling and frowning at the same time) is reliably linked to marital distress. One reason for this is that unhappy partners (typically expecting the worst from each other) tend to interpret mildly negative emotional messages as hostile and reciprocate with overtly hostile reactions. As this is reacted to in turn, destructive emotional sequences form an attack-and-defend spiral, typifying the tit-for-tat nature of many unhappy partnerships.

Living with another person can be difficult. Dealing with in-laws, jobs, careers, money, affection, leisure and children all take their toll and emotional intelligence can help with the cooperation and sensitivity needed in the relationship. In the pressure of daily life, however, conflict is almost inevitable. People are most likely to actually express anger not at the peak of their emotion but in situations where both partners have been feeling angry for some time. This is frequently in relationships where there is a longer-term climate of unhappiness or conflict, which may have built up but not been addressed. When couples are arguing, it's often easy to see that a partner is angry – but seeing *beyond* that can be the key to a good relationship. Seeing that someone is, for example, sad as well as angry can be difficult.

Evidence suggests that although 'insider knowledge' of one another might be expected to make it easier to read partners' feelings in relationships, it seems to be used selectively. Being able to see the emotion *causing* the anger can lead to reconciliation – and can even strengthen relationships. Recognizing genuine expressions of sadness or regret during a conflict can sometimes draw partners closer together, and it can enable them to break out of a climate of distrust.

In recent studies, couples in which both partners have low emotional intelligence were found to have significantly poorer relationships and happiness than partnerships involving either one or two partners with high EI. Whether the partnership involved one or two high-EI people made no significant difference.

Psychological contracts

Feelings that arise when people are angry or experience guilt, jealousy or love are profound emotions and show themselves repeatedly over time within relationships, depending on the type of relationship and the setting. But however the relationship was established in the first place, most involve some things which are open and defined (like where we live and our roles), and other things which are ill-defined or implicit (like the support we give to one another in times of trouble).

Emotional intelligence brings a very important focus to the implicit aspects of relationships. The expectations of members of a relationship can be described in terms of a 'psychological contract' that exists between its members. Based on the expectation that, over time, people can be trusted to fulfil their obligations to each other, relationships between individuals (or within teams for that matter) develop an expectation of reciprocity – if I do this, you will do that; if I behave this way toward you, you will respond in a broadly equal manner.

Amongst the many causes of breakdown in relationships, the loss of trust looms large. When employees feel that their manager is treating them badly, no matter what the circumstances, it is the breach of an implied contract of mutual support that causes the pain. The employer's behaviour implies a new contract in which he or she no longer seems to value the contribution of the employee, nor cares about their well-being.

Psychological contracts are more important in smaller settings – such as individual relationships and small groups. In these settings, building and maintaining equality and trust has been shown to be an essential precursor for continued and positive relationships.

Listening to the 'music'

In interpersonal relationships, maintaining good communication helps satisfy mutual expectations and helps the relationship to cope with current events and changes.

Have you ever tried the 'next table' game in a restaurant? It's really bad manners – and if it's all that fills your life every time you go to eat, it's really quite sad. But if like me you are fascinated by people, you might want to try it during a lull in your own erudite and meaningful conversation. The game consists of (without making it obvious) listening to how the people on the next table talk to each other and try to work out what the basis of their relationship is. You need to take a few surreptitious looks to check out a few nonverbal things – clothing, manner, gestures, eye contact, body posture, facial expressions – but the important skill in the game is to notice the unspoken positions being adopted, messages being implied or feelings being acted upon. In short, the 'music' that accompanies whatever is being said.

To find out how emotions, thinking and issues like power and influence are dealt with in every interaction between people, tune in to even the simplest of conversations. Discussions about shopping, family events, what's in the newspaper – even what to eat – sometimes go wrong for no apparent reason. Personal connections are often in the way: I heard someone beginning an emotional conversation recently by describing her annoyance at always having to go to *his* mother's for *both* Christmas *and* Boxing

Day. Difficulties like this continue until the underlying reasons are understood and discussed. But how this is done can build or diminish relationships. The response of the other party to an emotional issue is very telling.

If they don't feel that sufficient attention is being paid to their own needs, you often hear a spiral of conflict emerging, in which one statement (which might be perceived as threatening) is responded to by another, attacking and defending in turn. In the conversation mentioned above, the spiral continued, bringing in fairly threatening statements about other relatives, the rights of each person, what was done on other occasions and going all the way back to their wedding and what each person had expected from the other.

I waited for the breakdown point to be reached – the conversation descending into silence when neither party felt able (nor motivated) to continue. The only time feelings were referred to was an all-too-direct comment about his sense of being treated like a child which led to defensiveness and an angry response from his partner. The conversation was very quick, not allowing space to calm down nor, I suspect, even for them to understand the emotions that underpinned their situation.

People like people who like them. They will become more open and receptive when they receive positive feedback. People value what is sincere and real. So if a relationship is important to you, but it is not working well, showing your concern is essential. Even if there are blemishes, your feelings need to be explicit, not implied. Showing that you care about them will result in a more motivated and effective connection.

Emotions play an important but covert role in many conversations, influencing the relationship for some time afterwards.

Communication and groups

Most of us need to function in teams, companies, communities or family groups and there are many rewards for doing so. But being a member of a group isn't always easy. Communication can be difficult and there are some compromises we usually need to make. Understanding communications is an important part of emotional intelligence. There are many mechanical causes for communication going wrong (from noisy workplaces and poor telecommunication equipment), not to mention other problems like people being unable to express themselves, or feelings which they don't understand.

Communication difficulties are more often symptoms, rather than causes in their own right.

Such issues aside (and contrary to newspaper agony columns), communications problems in relationships are in themselves rarely causes of breakdown. There are some more fundamental issues, which emotional intelligence addresses.

Take someone joining a new team for example and the difficulty of 'fitting in'. Studies about groups and affiliation offer a wide variety of reasons for our need to fit in. People joining new teams are usually very sensitive to how they will be seen, what people think of them and how they need to act to get acceptance from new or influential people. The kind of emotional underworld which affects group life produces a variety of behaviours which many argue are inevitable whenever a group changes members.

What are some of the causes of emotional behaviour in groups? We all need to resolve a variety of problems arising when we enter new social situations:

- The problem of identity. Who am I to be in this team? Where do I fit in? What kind of behaviour is it acceptable for me to use?

- The problems of goals and needs. What do I want from this team? Can the group's goals be made consistent with my own? What can I offer the team?

- The problem of power, control and influence. Who controls what we do? How much power and influence can I have? What if I don't want the responsibility of leading?

- The problem of intimacy. How much can we trust each other? What do we do if there are breaches of trust? How can we increase the level of trust to what I need?

These problems produce a range of behaviours designed to establish 'fit'. However, they usually cause quite difficult problems because they are self-orientated – designed to help the individual establish their position:

- Dependency/counter-dependency. Leaning on or, alternatively, resisting anyone in the team who represents authority, especially the leader or the person representing the accepted values.

- Conflict and controlling. Asserting personal dominance, attempting to get their own way, regardless of the needs of others.

- Withdrawing. Trying to gain compliance via the sympathy of others, or simply trying to remove the source of uncomfortable feelings, by psychologically leaving the group.

- Pairing up. Seeking out one or two supporters and forming a kind of emotional sub-group in which members protect and support each other.

Skilful communication

One of the easiest aspects to observe about the way teams and groups function is their patterns of communication. What might you learn from observing the following?

- Who talks? For how long? How often?

- Who do people look at when they talk – potential supporters? Scanning the group? Perhaps no one looks at them and in turn they speak to empty space.

- Who talks after whom? Who interrupts whom?

- What style of communication is used? (Assertions? Tones of voice? Gestures?)

Empowering innovative people and creating rapport

Somebody once said that 'the only thing constant in life is change'. Throughout society in general, and industry in particular, changes are happening every day that will radically influence the way we do business tomorrow. The demand for creative innovation and for those who possess creativity is being seen at every level of management, marketing and productivity. The valuation at $104 billion of an eight-year-old company (Facebook) centred around programming developed by a Harvard student in his bedroom is staggering evidence of the importance of creativity and innovative people.

Studies have indicated that, although creative people are usually of above-average intelligence, above a certain level (IQ 120) there appears to be little correlation between creativity and IQ itself. Some researchers have found the link between creativity and academic performance to be negligible, as is the link between creativity and speed of thought. Unexpectedly, slow thinkers may be better at solving problems in an unexpected way than someone who thinks quickly. The reliability of psychometric tests for creativity is still limited, although there is increasing evidence that the link between divergent thinking (a richness of ideas from broad associations) and convergent thinking (narrowing ideas down to practicalities) is important. Some psychologists believe that the unconventional thinking found in many creative people is at least partly the result of some form of resistance to rigid rules. Creative individuals are often perceived as being somewhat rebellious and unwilling to give up their unique and singular nature.

Several factors appear to be critical to just how much creativity an individual presents:

- The level of creative talent in the individual
- The existence of other mental abilities or senses to nurture creativity (for example a graphic artist needs a strong visual memory and the ability to conceptualize)

- The background of the individual – depending on the creative field involved (science, consumerism, music, etc.), some environments may have stimulated, others stifled, their creative talents

- A work environment which minimizes overly rigid rules, criticism by peers or inflexible procedures.

EI characteristics of creativity are currently subject to considerable research activity, particularly by those exploring mixed and traits models of EI. Early indications are that both the presence and absence of certain EI characteristics may be important for creativity.

Research indicates that negative emotional states like stress are actually useful to perseverance with creativity, and positive EI characteristics like empathy and sociability were strongly linked to collaboration and aesthetics.

Metanoia and appreciative enquiry

Metanoia means changing your mindset. A word with a rich history, metanoia originally meant a fundamental shift of view, awakening a deeper and more fundamental awareness. It is an important concept for developing emotional intelligence; it can re-energize relationships, offer new ideas about people working together and give access to a rich vein of potential.

A good example of metanoia is the 'appreciative enquiry' approach to problem-solving. Changing your mind-set about how organizations operate can lead to new approaches. New thinking opens up creative possibilities. Traditionally, we tend to assume that organizations are full of problems that need to be solved; investigating them and identifying who and what is at fault equals problem-solving. People sometimes just mess up. By contrast, appreciative inquiry is an emotionally intelligent way to find changes and improvements. Based on changing the mindset from 'problem and fault focus' to 'developing the potential of what we have achieved', it is a cooperative search for the best in people, and their understanding about how to create positive change in the organization they have developed.

Appreciative enquiry has been used extensively in organizations facing major change (including in the health services and manufacturing industry), particularly when the commitment and energy of the staff must be maintained. Typically it goes through four stages – known as the four 'D's:

Discover: Appreciating and valuing the best of *what is*. Information and stories are gathered about what is working well.

Dream: Envisioning *what might be*. How do we want things to be for the future?

Design: Determining *what should be*. How can we move from where we are now to this vision of the future that we have created? How can we put the ideas into practice? Who will be involved?

Deliver: Innovating the new. In this phase, practical strategies or projects are put into practice and space created for ideas to flow and develop. There is an emphasis on empowering and encouraging people to take action and carry forward their own ideas.

A recent appreciative enquiry for developing a regional cancer strategy was undertaken in a complex healthcare setting, under great threat and with drastically limited resources. What would have previously taken months of meetings, committees and conflict was successfully completed over three sessions of an extended weekend workshop – just shows what you can do when you take an EI perspective.

The term metanoia is also about seeing the development of individuals in a broader way. It proposes that it is not enough for organizations merely to survive or cope. People need help to reduce their fears about a changing world and to help them define, creatively, new ways of being successful. To do that, we need to challenge boundaries and structures and develop widespread collaboration, awareness of how subtle changes build into big problems, understanding that procedures and systems limit what people can do, and a willingness to make big changes.

REMEMBER THIS!!! Metanoia is about opening up to new ways of looking at things and creating emotionally intelligent relationships – developing the rich vein of potential in most relationships.

Spotting skewed thinking

Skewed thinking can have serious effects on our relationships with others and our emotional health. Before talking about emotional intelligence recently to soldiers returning from deployment in Afghanistan, I spoke to the brigadier in charge of a major army charity. He talked about the difficulties facing returning soldiers who experience post-traumatic stress, and the effect it has on their sense of who they are. Discussing their reactions, the soldiers revealed a number of the defence mechanisms that we all use when our habits, our sense of self and our views of the world are all turned upside down.

Soldiers often create an unreal world at home, denying the traumas they have experienced. It can be a major problem for their families and close relationships. Difficult and upsetting thoughts can result in repression – unconsciously pushing anxiety-provoking information beyond our awareness; sometimes we react in ways which are the reverse of what we would normally think or do. Family problems are often caused by displacement, when traumatized military personnel redirect their emotions towards a less threatening 'object' like family members. Projecting their own, unacceptable thoughts on to others is some-times linked with a tendency to regress to times when they were younger and safer, resulting in regression to childlike behaviour, need for reassurance and even tantrums. The brigadier also commented on how often soldiers needed to rationalize their experience – substituting an accept-able reason in their own minds for actions and motives they might otherwise find unacceptable. The problem is, these defence mechanisms have consequences.

This emotional underworld may be extreme in compari-son to most of our lives but it serves to highlight errors of thinking which all of us can fall into without noticing. Stress, anxiety and difficult relationships can lead to forms of think-ing that make the world seem very dark and threatening. They are patterns of thinking, not individual thoughts, and they can obscure opportunities for new developments or making life better. The changes in thinking that we need to spot are outlined below; bear in mind that these may only be symptoms of a deeper emotional upset which has been experienced, perhaps a long time ago. Old habits die hard …

Types of skewed thinking
Over-generalization: eg. 'We *never* get *any* chance to do this right …'

Filtering: Focusing only on one aspect, excluding other, more positive aspects.

Discounting the positive: e.g. 'Yes I did better than anyone might have expected but *they didn't like me.*'

Absence of balance ('all-or-nothing thinking'): Something is either *right* or it's *wrong* – nothing in between.

Jumping to conclusions (future-ology): Thinking, 'This is what's *going to* happen' without sufficient information.

Magnification or minimization: Exaggerating the scale of something, e.g. 'It's the *end* of the world …'

Emotional reasoning: Basing judgements exclusively on feelings rather than evidence, e.g. 'I feel *guilty* – I must change what I decided.'

Blaming: e.g. 'It must be her *fault.*'

Mind reading and labelling: e.g. 'She *thinks that*; He's *like this*' (without evidence).

Personalization: Ego-centric behaviour in which it is difficult to focus on others, e.g. 'Everyone must be looking *at me*', 'What *I* did is …', '*My* thoughts are …'.

Our thoughts, beliefs and ways of interacting with others are based on the way we perceive what happens to us. How we do that is filtered when any of these types of skewed thinking are present. Being aware of skewed thinking is part of self-awareness – the first tool in the emotional intelligence skill set.

Noticing thinking biases in others is also an important aspect of building relationships. It is difficult to build positive and warm links with people if you have continual reason to suspect what they say, and when their thinking doesn't seem to follow the same rules as yours. Recognizing skewed thinking enables you to understand why you have problems and begin to build better relationships.

Mentalizing – how many friends do you have?

Building relationships with others is a key component of emotional intelligence in practice. There are many skills we can use to build strong and effective relationships with others. Some people are less comfortable with doing this though. We are not all gregarious, outgoing people, and making friends can be more difficult for some than others. As with so many aspects of human behaviour, it seems that the range of relationships that we have may, once again, be linked to the hard-wiring in our brains.

New research helps us to understand the mechanisms involved in our social and emotional intelligence. It highlights how the size of one part of the brain (the orbital prefrontal cortex, which is found just above the eyes) is linked to the number of friendships you develop. A study in 2012 found that individuals who had more friends had more capacity or 'neural volume' in this area, enabling them to do better at certain tasks associated with relationship-building.

This region is involved in a critical relationship-building tool: your ability to understand others' thinking. It is used to work out how to co-operate, to empathize, and to read others' body language. It is involved if we deceive people. It also enables us to accurately anticipate their behaviour, almost as if we had read their minds.

As young as eighteen months, infants look to a parent's face for information like 'How should I feel about that new person?' They seem to look for information about what the parent is thinking – is it frightening or not? At four, children can typically understand that people can have misunderstandings and false beliefs. Little Red Riding Hood really thought the wolf was her grandmother but the reader does not. Older children studying philosophy and ethics at school use mentalizing when discussing differing beliefs and attitudes across the world and contrasting them with their own. As adults, we use mentalizing every day, for example preparing presentations for an audience we haven't met. We use these skills when we buy a present for someone we care for, trying to get the perfect gift.

The 'theory of mind' (or the ability to 'mentalize') is 'one of the quintessential abilities that makes us human' according to Andrew Whiten, a leading psychologist and neuroscientist, talking about the ability to understand other people's thinking and reflecting on our amazing capacity for doing so.

Mentalizing means the ability to visualize what people may think and use it to behave effectively with others. Difficulty in this area is an important feature of people on

154

the autism spectrum and a condition called alexithymia, which is characterized by low emotional sensitivity and difficulty with relationships.

The neuroscience behind mentalizing involves the so-called mirror neurons which we discussed in relation to empathy. They activate a representation or memory of your own experience, which suggests to you what someone's intentions *might* be. Our frontal cortex then decides if the imaginary representation is relevant. This is an important survival skill based on instinct and experience, and because intention relates to some future action, the level of emotional processing is low.

As we discussed in relation to empathy, where there is significant emotion (like happiness, fear, disgust or attraction) a different process is used. The same mirror neurons (using signals like facial expressions, voice tones, speech and gestures in the other person) create the representation and memories in you of what the other person might be experiencing.

But instead of linking to the cortex to understand it, the brain uses areas more involved with creating emotional reactions in your body. These include the amygdala and a place in the older, mammalian brain concerned with survival and safety known as the insula. These two areas create intense images, drawing on *your* real emotions. Your experience of mentalizing becomes more intense.

KEY TERM

In short, **mentalizing** is the ability to understand the perspectives and attitudes of others, their beliefs, values and emotions. Your emotional intelligence helps you understand how people's ideas relate to each other and uses connections between them as the basis for relationship-building.

Understanding how people are feeling is an important aspect of emotional intelligence. But you always need to remember that empathy is created from your own experience and memories – so while you think you understand someone else's emotions, you may not always be right.

PART II: EMOTIONAL INTELLIGENCE IN PRACTICE

5. EI and the workplace

The added value of EI

Daniel Goleman's 1995 book *Emotional Intelligence* was described in the introduction as a smash hit which popularized the developing field of EI. In subsequent years, much of the interest in emotional intelligence has been driven by its application to the workplace. The continuing interest in EI has been stoked in later years, particularly by the speed of change affecting markets and business organizations since the millennium, and the acknowledgement that technology has heralded such increasing complexity that old forms of control and command management are unsustainable.

Developments driving continued interest in emotional intelligence include:

- Structural changes like flatter structures and rationalization/downsizing
- Changing product life cycles
- Increasing complexity and the job design implications of technology
- Market changes, globalization and financial adjustments

- Unprecedented growth in the not-for-profit and values-based sector
- Continual change and continuous process review
- Need for enhanced performance
- Insufficient capacity or resource shortages
- Employment patterns changing and frequency of job changes within a career
- Increased stress and mental health issues
- Consumerism affecting aspirations
- Increasing focus on customer relationships.

To balance the demands of the customers and products with the demands of the technology and systems used to deliver them is difficult enough. However, the most expensive resource in most organizations is the staff. Emotional intelligence is one way of ensuring that working together effectively can create added value. There are many hidden areas of human interaction in organizations and they all need to work if the organization is to be sustained.

The concept of emotional intelligence found fertile ground in the changing landscape of workplace organizations. The idea of a 'learning organization' was defined in 1990 by Peter Senge, emphasizing the emotional aspects of organizations. Arguing for better relationships based on shared vision and values, he has succeeded in encouraging organizations to take a fresh perspective, to understand how people in the organization see themselves and others and the mental models they use to understand how things work. Emotional intelligence has been identified by many organizations as vital for growth and sustainability. Relationships with customers and stakeholders are vital and EI helps build 'connectedness' between staff, customers, stakeholders and the wider community of which it is part.

Visible aspects
Strategies
Objectives
Policies and procedures
Structure
Technology
Formal authority
Chains of command

Hidden aspects
Attitudes
Perceptions
Group norms
Informal interactions
Interpersonal and
intergroup conflicts

Visible and invisible aspects of human interaction

Effective leaders look beyond themselves, at others; they control their reactions and skilfully manage their relationships. Under their leadership, other employees work effectively with colleagues and have strong relationships with customers and stakeholders.

Emotional intelligence has been used in organizations with effective leadership to communicate goals, values and ways of working that are positive, authentic, value people and embrace change.

The growing importance of emotional intelligence

An increasing body of research shows EI to be a major factor in successful performance, particularly in sales and management. Results indicate, of course, that other factors are important: resourcing affects performance; marketing of products influences the response of customers. But an objective review of the research strongly suggests that selling to customers, or negotiating and influencing *requires* emotional intelligence for them to be performed well.

Job skills like assertiveness, negotiation and people management are *underpinned* by emotional intelligence. Because of this, many researchers into emotional intelligence in the workplace use the phrase **emotional competences** to describe the skills needed in specific job situations.

In 2000, one of many studies reviewed 358 managers to assess if there are specific leadership competencies that distinguish high performers from average performers. The study revealed a strong relationship between top-performing leaders and the emotional competences of self-awareness, self-management, social awareness and social skills. This finding supports similar conclusions, by David McClelland, covering 30 different organizations.

In this study, men and women did not seem to differ in the level of EI they possessed, although they differed on specific aspects of it. Women scored significantly higher on interpersonal skills and social responsibility, while men were more self-aware, being better at managing their emotions and more adaptable. Women were more aware of emotions, particularly in situations with two or more people, and were more able to demonstrate empathy towards others. Men scored better on self-reliance, assertiveness, stress tolerance and impulse control.

From a corporate point of view, Apple computers' rocky sales and low market share during the early 1990s was transformed by design flair and the marketing brilliance brought by Steve Jobs when he returned to the company in 1996. There is little evidence about his personal emotional intelligence but as an early management change, the company moved towards an emotionally intelligent corporate strategy. It focused on the affection, loyalty and engagement his customers held for Apple, their emotional attachment to novel and creative technology and the importance of their instincts and feelings towards design. The company used these factors as criteria for decision-making, engaging customers in the development process and targeting marketing at achieving emotional responses to products. The strategy resulted in an increase in annual revenues of $60 billion.

The ability both to identify feelings and to handle stress through self-management is another aspect of emotional intelligence that has been found to be important for success. A comparison of managers in a retail DIY chain found that those with greater ability to handle stress (both personally and within their teams) were able to achieve higher profitability, fewer industrial relations problems, more sales per square foot, more sales per employee, and a greater return on investment.

As outlined in Part I, empathy is another important aspect of emotional intelligence. Recent surveys of retail buyers in the UK and South Africa have identified the importance of characteristics related to empathy in sales representatives. When the buyers' orders were analysed, 30 per cent more value was given to the sales reps that scored highly on the EI characteristics of sensitivity, awareness, imagination, the ability to express feelings and openness to changing their behaviour. The buyers' explanations of their ordering decisions confirm that high EI scores translate into the reps' behaviour. The buyers' perceptions were that they listened well and really understood the buyers' wants, needs and concerns. They showed that they were responsive to how buyers were feeling and were keen to create a sense of openness about themselves and the company they represented.

Emotional intelligence increases turnover.
- Optimists outsell pessimists by up to 25 per cent.
- Buyers rewarded sales people with empathy by ordering 30 per cent more by value.

In the military workplace, studies have shown that the most effective leaders for operational units tend to be warmer (with a good sense of humour), express how they feel, look for/understand reactions amongst their colleagues and behave in a sociable way. In education and social care organizations, the ability to openly express feelings whilst maintaining self-control has enabled team leaders to establish better relationships with both colleagues and clients, leading to improved co-operation, acceptance of constraints, improved performance and collaborative behaviour-sharing resources.

Emotional intelligence is about knowing when and how to *express* emotion, as well as controlling it.

In a 2001 study, supermarket staff in the UK who had high levels of EI were found to have less stress and perform better; they were happier, had a better home/work balance and enjoyed better health.

Police research reported similar findings in 2004, with greater emotional awareness linked to being able to handle stress in their jobs better.

You might not see yourself as a 'people person' but the weight of evidence is clear. The 'social system' (leadership, decision-making, motivation, culture, values, etc.) needs to integrate with the technical and production systems you use. A workplace managed without emotional intelligence is going to be an unhappy and unsuccessful place.

Coping with uncertainty

Sometimes it's important to state the obvious. In the day-to-day routines of modern business life, emotional intelligence is not a magic wand to be waved, expecting that it will resolve any and all problems. Take for example one of the constant problems faced by all organizations: how to deal with the need for change.

What do you think were the benefits of each action taken by the manager in the following case study?

An NHS Trust manager in charge of a severely overspending hospital unit needed to introduce major changes, reduce expenditure, increase reliability of technology and conform to nationally imposed service targets. Her predecessor had recommended swingeing cuts.

The new manager adopted a more EI-informed approach. She asked the staff to identify and collect data to review work processes, the overall demand for the service and its current capacity. She gave a representative group of clinicians and others the authority to make changes themselves. She employed a facilitator to work with the group to overcome any difficulties in working together.

The emotionally intelligent approach was developed in part by trying to establish a clearer vision of what was possible in the service and the values that needed to be shared, and also a positive spirit about what needed to be done. So over the following six months they worked on specific guiding values, rationalizing goals, and co-operation for better alignment of patient journeys. They developed an internal social networking IT system to boost communication and information about the potential impact of upcoming changes.

At the end of seven months, they had achieved all nationally set standards for patient treatment times, reduced overall costs by six per cent, were in the midst of changing many patient and management processes and were running weekly updates both on clinical matters and on impending policy changes. Psychological well-being questionnaires issued at the start and end of the project showed an increase in satisfaction of 27 per cent, despite the redundancy effect of two per cent of the staff being transferred to another service unit.

In this hospital, the initial focus on savings had been so great that the effect on staff was underestimated. Communicating and giving the staff responsibility for change based on a clear set of values ensured that anxiety was reduced and the changes were implemented. The manager recognized the importance of maintaining stability by improving communication within the team.

Emotional intelligence in the approach tackled the disabling effects of uncertainty, and increased the ownership of change. It reduced anxiety about future change by increasing communication and establishing channels of intelligence. The 'metanoia' approach prompted them to rationalize ambiguous and conflicting goals and think of effective procedures to continue achieving their values and mission.

Difficult situations in your workplace

What do you find to be the most difficult situations at work?

List two or three situations you have experienced in the last week or two. How did they manifest themselves at the start?

What were the events or factors involved that kick-started your awareness of these as difficult situations?

What were your initial thoughts about the difficulties? (There might have been a rush of many thoughts – just list the ones which made you feel particularly uncomfortable.)

Think about similar situations in the past – it might be helpful to think about your problem as a system of interrelated parts. Is there any way in which they all connect up?

Try to describe what you think the root causes for the situation are.

Try to describe what you think might be the root causes for you seeing it as a difficult situation. What are the consequences? Have you experienced similar situations before?

Are you doing any 'skewed thinking'? (See pages 151–152. List any you recognize.)

The emotional rollercoaster of difficult situations

Dealing with unreasonable colleagues, rude customers, annoying emails, frustrating decisions and unpredictable behaviour is, for many people, a typical day at work. Difficult situations at work produce a similar rollercoaster to the way people experience tension in any stressful situation.

Surprise and uncertainty, which may be the beginning of a difficult situation, mark a period of strong arousal (the body's response to threat, as described in Part I). This continues until action to resolve it begins.

The response is triggered in the brain's limbic system, structures in the brain which, amongst other things, have a major effect on how we deal with emotional situations. The impact of the situation on our emotions is modified to some extent by the cognitive activity (analysis and thinking) which takes place. But the power of the emotions increases as the awareness of the situation's potential consequences are understood. The tension we experience is maintained until the possibility of developing a satisfactory solution begins to take shape. The arousal (tension) reduces when action is taken and the situation looks like being resolved.

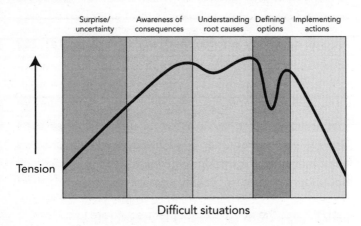

The emotional rollercoaster

In the normal, day-to-day workplace, difficult situations are almost inevitable and are best handled with emotional stability and calm. The mistake that some people make when they hear about EI is thinking that staying in control means shutting down or trying to be unemotional. Of course there are occasions when it is important to react to what happens in a dispassionate way. But that's not really the point. Emotional intelligence isn't about creating zombies!

 Mindfulness promotes emotion to make it part of the conscious thought process. This reduces the tension you experience and helps you to understand others' feelings too.

When a new, difficult situation arises, your levels of stress may have been already quite high. It is important to recognize that your judgement in your workplace may be influenced by the argument you had with your partner before leaving home. Perhaps reinforced by your grumpiness all morning and an earlier meeting with difficult colleagues, the accumulated irritation can make you much more sensitive to difficult situations than you would wish to be. You know about self-awareness and mindfulness from Part I of this book but the point is that other people are just like you. Their reaction may be influenced by other experiences or pressures.

Handling these situations begins with working out what emotions are present, why, and what the consequences might be: an upset customer may be furious about being treated badly and might cancel their order, but they may also react very cautiously the next time one of your sales reps call, even if it is a different person. The person upset about having his telephone calls ignored might become more demanding in future. Or he may simply turn to another supplier. And most probably, the busy sales rep that ignored the call may have difficulty closing future sales. It is from a starting point of being aware of the emotions and their possible consequences that an emotionally intelligent person acquires the power to handle the situation. You can then decide the best way to manage the relationship from there.

EI for difficult situations involves:

- Developing a positive perspective focusing on strengths and opportunities rather than blame and weakness
- Being aware of your gut reactions
- Using empathy – a key indicator of emotional intelligence
- Decoding body language
- Showing others that you understand their feelings
- Checking with them that you understand the problem
- Being clear about the endgame – solutions that satisfy both needs
- Gaining attention
- Collaborative language and problem-solving
- Providing the basis for positive future work.

Anxiety

For some people, the obstacles they face in dealing with difficult situations aren't the actual situation itself but their own anxieties and fears. Anyone who has experienced a panic attack (say, about flying) knows only too well the dread and fear which accompanies it. But subsequently the flying isn't the focus. The problem becomes fear of the panic attack itself, driven by the powerlessness that goes with it. Subsequently, any thought of flying is defined by panic and feeling trapped. It makes dealing with the situation itself (the flight) doubly difficult. In work situations too, engaging in 'future-ology' – speculating what *might* happen and the *imagined* consequences of our fears – results in what is sometimes called 'anticipatory anxiety'.

Take someone who fears they will perform badly speaking to a difficult group. The fear may lead to procrastination – putting off preparing, for example, to minimize anxiety – and consequently a self-fulfilling prophecy, i.e. the fear of performing badly actually causing it to happen.

An aware, emotionally intelligent individual will acknowledge their fears, accepting that everyone gets worried from time to time. Over the longer term, emotionally intelligent people tend to become self-confident, purposeful individuals with a greater tolerance for stress, so accepting feelings of anxiety and acknowledging their legitimacy doesn't mean letting them take control.

Your awareness of the others who are involved helps you to distinguish between the substantive problem and the people issues involved. Understanding behaviour gives you issues you may need to explore or options for how problems can be resolved.

Managing yourself in this situation requires problem-solving skills: the ability to distinguish symptoms of a problem from underlying causes; a sense of how much of the problem you can tackle (the boundaries of what you can deal with); whether you need a plan and how to deal with any emotions present in you.

Leadership, emotional intelligence and success

Today's new economy is one in which the speed of communication has increased phenomenally, both internally and with markets at home and abroad. Internet trading, social networking and the fundamental restructuring of both products and the markets they are traded in has led to major organizational shifts. As layers of middle management disappear, senior management overheads are beginning to be trimmed. Collaborative partnerships and outplacement have replaced old-fashioned command and control hierarchies and organizations are demanding that people work cheaper, faster and smarter than ever before. Survival post-financial crash has focused attention on the need for growth and innovation.

The consequence of this organizational and market instability for employees is a widespread perception of a more threatening environment and greater awareness of risk. The relationship between employees and leaders has also changed in this environment. Whereas in times of success, staff look for freedom and opportunities to take on change and challenge (and actively reject being too closely managed), these circumstances are very different. In some organizations, employees have a tendency to avoid risk, contrasting with the positive and proactive approach needed in new situations. Today's internal company environment typically involves an increase in working hours, more technological complexity, higher levels of insecurity and work imperatives that can lead to problems with work/life balance, which is also an important issue for long-term survival.

Increasingly, employees now look to their managers and leaders for the encouragement and support for taking on new challenges. Emotionally intelligent leaders are strongly aware of the need to respond to the anxieties of their staff and re-establish the positive emotional connection with purpose and direction of the organization.

A study by the Centre for Creative Leadership recently found two critical areas in which leadership seems to fail in this context. Leaders who are unable to adapt themselves to change often become rigid as a way of minimizing uncertainty and risk. They may be unable either to hear the concerns of staff or to respond sufficiently quickly to the changes which the new conditions may require. They also unwittingly foster poor relationships. They alienate those they work with by becoming too harshly critical, insensitive, overly demanding or manipulative. Those leaders, to be effective, need to become more emotionally intelligent.

According to that research, for senior leadership positions, emotional intelligence competencies are more than 85 per cent of what sets star performers apart from the average. And the higher you go in the organization, the more these competencies are seen to matter. In a study of the financial impact of emotional intelligence, two years after assessing how often they demonstrated their emotional intelligence and the financial benefits it created, 41 per cent of experienced leaders who developed frequent emotional intelligence behaviours were promoted, compared with only 10% of those who didn't. At least from a career development point of view, emotional intelligence is significant for success! But what evidence is there about how emotionally intelligent behaviour influences success across the range of functions in an organization?

The table opposite shows the emotional intelligence behaviours which are associated with high performance and career success in a number of different professions:

The research in this area suggests that, overall, the characteristics which appear to foster success across all occupational settings are:

- Leaders who feel that they are both developing themselves and fulfilling their potential
- People who feel that their relationships contribute to feeling happy for more than 75 per cent of their time
- Leaders who can view their colleagues and the situations they face with optimism

Prevalent EI behaviours	Star performers from:						
	Marketing	Customer service	Sales	HR	Finance	Senior management	Legal
Optimism	✓		✓	✓	✓		
Reality testing	✓		✓			✓	
Independence	✓						✓
Impulse control	✓						
Social responsibility		✓		✓			✓
Stress tolerance		✓	✓				
Assertiveness		✓	✓	✓			✓
Happiness		✓		✓	✓	✓	
Interpersonal relationships	✓	✓		✓	✓	✓	✓
Self-actualization		✓		✓	✓	✓	
Self-regard			✓			✓	
Empathy			✓		✓		✓

- People who are confident and positive about themselves and who actively seek feedback from others
- Individuals who are assertive and prepared to voice dissent, should the need arise.

6. Parenting and teaching children

Emotional literacy

The promotion of emotional health and well-being in schools has been a concern for teachers for many years. Work in schools on this has rarely been defined as being about emotional intelligence, despite the parallels in the topics involved and development aims. A report by the UK government in 2005 linked the use of EI learning materials provided nationally to two areas of education:

1. Promoting social and emotional well-being, to deal effectively with issues of pupils' mental health.

2. Pupils' behaviour – kids do not necessarily know how to behave well. Some will not have had the opportunity to learn good behaviour at home; others may be learning it, but their skills need reinforcing.

The general significance of children being taught to be emotionally literate is clear. A child or student (or anyone else for that matter) who is anxious, angry or depressed won't learn easily: people who are in these states do not take in information efficiently or deal with it well. When emotions overwhelm concentration, what is being swamped is the mental capacity that cognitive scientists call 'working memory', i.e. the ability to hold in mind all the information you need, relevant to the task in hand. The impact of this can certainly be limiting for the development of skills and potential but has also been seen to be encouraging a sense of disaffection with school, society at large and socially accepted norms of behaviour.

Research into the role of emotional intelligence in shaping behaviour at school found that pupils who scored higher in emotional intelligence were less likely to have difficulties at school. A number of studies suggest that lower emotional intelligence is implicated in unacceptable behaviour, so on this basis, it seems reasonable to suggest that developing children's emotional intelligence will help to develop a more inclusive environment and reduce the number of children at risk of disaffection.

Other clinical research points to the risks resulting from *ignoring* emotional intelligence. The presence of callous and unemotional traits in young people, particularly in boys, seems to confer a subsequent vulnerability to mental health problems over and above those which might be a product of the established risk factors for childhood psychiatric illness. Research is currently under way about how these traits develop and how EI modifies the risks which result.

A tale of looting and imprisonment
In 2011, a wave of rioting and looting took place in several UK cities. A nineteen-year-old student with no previous involvement in crime entered

a broken shop window in London and stole a stereo worth £150. Imprisoned for three months, he described being involved in all the 'hype and energy of the crowd', 'feeling that he had no way out of the crowd' and being so excited he just 'didn't think', picked up a box and ran. He just 'wasn't himself', he alleged, and didn't even know what he had taken. He already had the same stereo at home.

Police reports say that although he understood right from wrong, he found it difficult to remember anything that happened and appeared not to understand why he had been arrested. He was a community volunteer and the behaviour was completely out of character.

He repeatedly says now, 'I just wasn't thinking straight – the thing I most regret is doing something when I was out of control. I couldn't handle the hype.'

So what do we want for our children?

More than ten years ago in *Defying Disaffection*, American researcher Reva Klein set out an agenda for education which fits the model of emotional intelligence exactly: 'We want our children to be able to learn how to communicate their feelings, set themselves goals and work towards them, interact successfully with others, resolve conflicts peaceably, control their anger and negotiate their way through the many complex relationships in their lives today and tomorrow.'

This means helping all pupils, from the beginning of their education, to have purposeful goals, manage strong feelings, resolve conflict effectively and fairly, solve problems, work and play cooperatively, and be respectful, calm, optimistic and resilient. But are social, emotional and behavioural skills 'taught or caught'?

 Emotional intelligence is a key factor in helping children to learn effectively and making their classrooms a calm and optimistic place for learning.

Teaching emotional intelligence

In both the UK and US, many teachers focus on five key aspects to learning social, emotional and behavioural skills:

1. Self-awareness
2. Managing feelings
3. Motivation
4. Empathy
5. Social skills.

Following professional and government interest in emotional intelligence, many schools now have structured programmes for teaching these skills to children within the curriculum. But the settings in which schools operate are also important. Emotional intelligence is not something that can be taught in isolation. It needs to be 'caught' from others. Children need to support their learning by practice in real-life situations and an emotionally positive environment where emotional intelligence is modelled and children coached routinely and consistently.

There is now a considerable body of evidence which suggests that if this environment is in place, learning emotional intelligence can benefit both academic performance and behaviour in schools. Evaluations of UK programmes indicate a linear increase in children's mathematical ability and significant positive impact in languages and in arts and social science subjects. For example, in one study, students were better able to understand the motives of characters being studied in English literature and history.

From a behaviour and attendance point of view, an analysis of UK initiatives reveals those children who achieved *high* scores on emotional intelligence:

- exhibited fewer negative behaviours and emotions at school

- were less likely to let their difficulties interfere with their peer relations and classroom learning

- were less likely to experience negative emotional states, hyperactivity problems or behavioural problems with their peers

- were less likely to have temper tantrums, lie and cheat

- were generally obedient and worked well with authority

- were less distracted, more able to concentrate, stay on task and think things through before acting

- were more likely to form friendships and to be liked by peers

- were less likely to pick on or bully their peers

- were rated by their teachers as being considerate of others' feelings (demonstrated in such behaviours as sharing with other children, being kind to younger children, being helpful if someone is hurt and volunteering to help others).

Children who achieved *low* scores on emotional intelligence, however, had more problems. They often complained of headaches, had many worries, were often unhappy, down-hearted or tearful, were nervous or clingy in new situations, had many fears and were easily scared. They seemed not to have developed effective coping strategies to help them deal with school difficulties, challenging situations nor any typical classroom or peer problems that might arise.

Different origins, same answers

Research in the US and in the UK has led to teaching strategies which promote EI in schools and the development of materials both for teacher training and for classroom use. In the UK, the origin of the approach taken was professional concerns about the social aspects of schools, in particular relating to attendance and behaviour. In the US, however, the initial focus was on whether EI benefits academic achievement. It would appear that it does. The approaches in both the US and UK now focus on a similar range of issues and skills.

A challenge for teachers?

A paper published by the UK government in 2001 ('Achieving Success in Schools') described the importance of working on the emotional intelligence of children. EI was seen in that paper as an important vehicle for promoting positive, collaborative behaviour that would result in more effective learning and better creativity. Improved emotional intelligence, the paper argued, could lead to improved levels of achievement across the whole curriculum.

As described above, the importance of the ability to recognize, understand, handle and appropriately express emotions has become widely accepted in teaching. In his *The Little Book of Big Stuff about the Brain*, consultant paediatric neurologist Andrew Curran discusses emotional literacy and the argument that, as their brains develop, children have to acquire increasing amounts of independence and resilience to support the growth of neural connections. Arguing for teaching methods which encourage more self-knowledge and control of their actions by pupils, he describes the growing awareness of emotional intelligence in teaching to be 'the most important thing to have happened in education for the last hundred years.'

Emotional literacy and the social or emotional intelligence on which it is based can be of great importance for what teachers teach, how the curriculum is designed, the way lessons are delivered, the relationships teachers develop with their pupils and, perhaps ultimately, the results that students are able to achieve.

In countries such as the UK where, since 2001, the need to develop emotional intelligence within the education system has been accepted at government level, guidance is provided for teachers and other school workers, focusing on helping children to:

- Take responsibility for, and be able to manage, their own learning
- Develop the habits of effective learning
- Know how to work independently, without close supervision
- Be confident and able to investigate problems and find solutions
- Be resilient in the face of difficulties
- Be creative, inventive, enterprising and entrepreneurial.

These outcomes are achieved by using skills such as identifying, handling and expressing emotions; anger and anxiety management; building self-esteem; and developing social skills through the friendship offered in classes and schools.

The key challenge for teachers is not how they organize specific emotional intelligence classes; rather it is whether they can integrate learning about emotional intelligence into the teaching of their normal subjects – for example, incorporating learning about self-awareness, managing emotions, empathy and other such skills into a maths, geography, science or language class.

THINK ABOUT IT Good teachers have been concerned about developing thinking skills for many years and how they do this is vital. If you are a teacher, how does emotional intelligence feature in your personal approach to day-to-day teaching?

- How do you encourage a pupil to be aware of their emotions when they are finding a piece of work difficult?

- How do you encourage a pupil to manage their own feelings when their behaviour or performance is affected?

- How do you give feedback so that the individual pupil is aware of what they can achieve and values him- or herself?

- How do you help a child who is frustrated, uncertain or anxious? And how do you spot them in the first instance?

- How much importance do you place on the social process of group work, rather than task performance?

- Where differences in view exist between pupils, how do you reward collaboration rather than the correct answer?

- Where do social, emotional and behavioural skills feature in your schemes of work or lesson plans?

- How are your strategies for managing feelings employed in day-to-day curriculum work, rather than in behaviour or discipline situations?

Parenting

The housemaster at my old school always used a pointed remark to get parents thinking about their roles in the development of their children. He often said to them, 'Education and learning is too important to leave it to the school, however good it is.' He believed that the foundation of what we now call a child's emotional intelligence begins with the child's early relationship with its parents. His challenge would be to ask parents or carers, 'What do you do now to lay a solid foundation for later development?'

 Here are a few thoughts about positive parenting to develop your child's emotional intelligence. Which do you feel comfortable with, and which might cause you some difficulty?

1. High EI starts in infancy with your child's earliest inter-actions with you, from which they develop feelings of security and trust. Spend time with your infant when they need you. Respond quickly to their cries. Help the infant to feel secure by gradually distancing yourself (for example at night-time). Avoid the recommendation to 'Let them cry – they'll get over it.'

2. Almost 100 years ago, psychologist H. Stack Sullivan demonstrated that infants pick up anxiety from their parents. Recent research has confirmed that parents' touch, voices and movements can either soothe a child or stimulate anxiety. Make sure you deal with your own anxiety and stress; don't communicate it to the young child.

3. Babies learn to calm themselves by first having some-one else soothe them, then responding in a mirrored way. From this they gain the experience of managing and tolerating their physical and emotional needs. The groundwork for self-calming later in life comes from this; showing the infant how to calm themselves by holding them, soothing and stroking helps the neural networks develop in the right way. It needs to begin early in life because as they get older, their emotions affect them more intensely. As toddlers, they have a very hard time learning to self-soothe or self-regulate, because every feeling makes them anxious. In later childhood, feel-ings of neediness, fear or anger can trigger sweeping

anxiety or even panic, and without the ability to manage them, behaviours like bullying, avoidance and non-cooperation will ensue.

4. Teach kids that they can't choose their feelings any more than they can choose their arms and legs, but they can – and must – choose what to do with those feelings. Little ones can't differentiate between their emotions and their selves so it is important that younger children understand boundaries to define what actions are acceptable to others – and what actions are not. But you won't get through to an emotional child unless you accept and affirm what they are feeling first.

5. Don't try to diminish what they feel, and listen to your child's feelings. Saying things like 'A little scratch like that doesn't hurt' or 'Big boys don't cry' might be OK for you but doesn't help a child self-manage their hurt. Acknowledge, empathize, let them show you what happened, help them to understand that things will get better in time, give them a little time to process what they are feeling so that then they'll be ready to move on.

6. Disapproving of their fear or anger won't stop them from having those feelings, but it may well force them to repress them. Repression doesn't work. Repressed feelings don't fade away as they do when they have been freely expressed. They look for a way out and

can be the root cause of behaviour problems in later childhood.

7. Show you understand the child's feelings by describing what you see and reflecting their behaviour back to them (for example, 'You seem very angry with your sister tonight'). Accepting their feelings and reflecting them back does not mean you agree with or endorse the feelings. You will probably defuse the situation and kick-start the self-management process. Acknowledge your child's perspective and empathize.

8. Help your child learn to problem-solve. When the emotional charge of a situation begins to dissipate, the use of logic and thinking reinforces the return to normality. Problem-solving might need some support from you but resist the urge to handle the problem yourself.

9. Children use adults as role models and will replicate the approach and behaviour they see in you. Are you aware of how you are feeling and do you acknowledge it? How do you deal with your own feelings when under stress? How do you show your understanding about what others are feeling? Can you stay calm during emotionally charged discussions? Do you empathize when feelings are expressed? Modelling emotional intelligence is an important way to help children develop.

10. One of the most important skills you can help your child to develop is how to handle anger constructively. They

will learn what you model. Use words, not force. Discuss what is beneath your anger. Don't let it escalate. Keep listening to them and make sure your emotions stay in control. If necessary, use deep breathing to help you.

11. One of the most difficult things your child may have to deal with is a physical difference: say, an absent father, a learning disability, being adopted, an impending divorce, or a relative who abuses alcohol or drugs. Every child has things that he or she is afraid to talk about. And those are the issues on which they most need your support and guidance. Feelings of inadequacy or fear, absence of loved ones, actions by family members which are not properly understood – all these things can be difficult to discuss. You can help develop emotional intelligence by showing that difficult feelings can be talked about. You might talk to your child about things that you find difficult, for example.

Parenting styles of mothers and fathers

Parents' lives become very busy. Devoting time for the emotional development of your child shouldn't take less priority, but it often does.

Research in Spain, the US and the UK has demonstrated that the time mothers spend with their children has a significant influence on their emotional development. The more time spent interacting with their mother, doing things which have an education element (like visiting museums or creating stories or pieces of art), the more emotional intelligence develops. Time spent watching TV together, however, does not appear to have this effect.

A controlling type of parenting and a harsh or disciplinary approach negatively influences development of EI, whilst a more democratic and thoughtful approach has been found to encourage greater emotional stability and flexibility. Encouraging the child to take responsibility both in what they do and in the household more generally positively influences their ability to understand others' emotions, to be responsible in social situations and to establish good interpersonal relationships.

The role of fathers in developing a child's EI seems to be influenced by the degree to which they conform to cultural stereotypes of male behaviour. Research indicates that 'macho' approaches correlate with low development of emotional intelligence, whereas fathers who emphasize the behaviour and characteristics described in the preceding pages achieve similar results to mothers.

Fathers with high levels of emotional intelligence display more pleasure responses to their children's positive behaviour and less anger to their negative behaviour. As a result, they are well suited to build self-esteem, inspire confidence and foster positive behaviour in their children by using positive reinforcement.

These studies show that EI can be nurtured and improved by positive parenting styles. Positive parenting styles are characterized by involvement with the child, a democratic way of decision-making, an emphasis on accountability, moderate autonomy for the child, a thoughtful use of discipline and a tendency to emphasize independence more than being child-absorbed.

 Emotionally intelligent rules for parenting are:

- Spend time with your child.

- Establish rules that you all (you, your child, other family members) agree to, to inform decision-making.

- Allow moderate autonomy for the child to decide how they should act.

- Find ways to define the responsibilities which accompany their freedom.

- Discipline that is fair and takes circumstances into account.

- Encourage independence.

---

7. Emotional intelligence and health

The psychological immune system

Emotional intelligence, with its emphasis on managing your own emotions as well as the interaction with others, is of real benefit in helping to protect people from stress, anxiety and depression, as well as promoting a positive frame of mind. But the impact appears to be rather wider than mental health; EI is also important with regard to your physical health. It is around 100 years since the relationship between physiological events and emotional feelings began to be explored. What was to become the 'James–Lange theory' was followed by the 'Cannon–Bard' and later 'Schachter–Singer' theories, all of which demonstrated strong links between body processes and emotions.

Immunity

Our immune system is a complex community of systems, cells and barriers that protect us from disease-causing organisms. Research indicates that feelings (that is, the bio-chemical response our bodies make to our perceptions and emotions), and sometimes the psychological sensations they create, trigger an immune response. This is our ability to provide rapid antibody responses to invading pathogens or changes that affect our internal systems and organs.

As long ago as 1936, Hans Selye provided evidence that the adrenal cortex, the immune system and the gut were all connected and altered by hypertrophy (enlargement of cells) of the adrenal glands. It showed that the connections were altered by the effects of emotion and prolonged stress. The consequence of this for the digestive system has now been identified as irritable bowel syndrome.

A recent study using neuroimaging has backed up the significance of emotional perception as a real entity. When individuals are psychologically injured by social exclusion felt as rejection, the pain registers in the same area of the brain as physical pain. This suggests a possible physical foundation of our consciousness and that emotions have a physiological role.

Just as the biological immune system is geared up to detect dangerous micro-organisms, the psychological immune system is geared up to stimulate our bodies to detect dangerous elements in the environment and to seek opportunities to avoid them. Our built-in alertness to threats on life, physical well-being, property, possessions, and our sense of self and identity, and our emotional reactions to risks, constitute the essence of the psychological components of our immune system which are integrated with our biological systems.

For this reason, the threats and dangers we face always take priority in our awareness. We are programmed to look for them. You become aroused when you hear a loud, unfamiliar noise, see a flash of light, feel something crawling on your skin, smell smoke within your home or find your child coming home in tears. These situations reach one's awareness in a hurry, and when they do, we react intuitively. Later, however, we draw up plans to deal with them based on our experience, knowledge, superstitions and beliefs. So, although we are stuck with a protective system that scans the horizon for threats, danger and opportunities, we are not stuck with responses that are encased in cement. Our emotional intelligence provides both opportunities to engage successfully with others and to cope with the physiological changes and effects that threat and risk can trigger.

 Part of your immune system is a feelings-driven, biochemical process governed by our perceptions. Our health and ability to stay healthy are intimately connected to the way we manage our emotions.

Rumination and anxiety

Recent Australian studies have shown that people's satisfaction with their lives, their psychological well-being, and particularly their levels of anxiety, are determined by factors like emotional self-control and self-knowledge described in Part I of this book. For example, people prone to rumination have trouble getting upsetting thoughts out of their minds and are absorbed with thoughts about the past or future. This leads to inertia – not taking action to change their situation – and avoiding unpleasant feelings by trying to 'reason away' the uncontrollable.

From a health perspective, these long-term studies have established that people who engage in more rumination have higher levels of depression over time, exhibit symptoms of mental health problems and need medical treatment more often. Ruminators have difficulty responding to family, friends and others, believing them to be providing less relevant help than they need, raising important issues for long-term care and patient recovery. High rumination has also been associated with delayed recovery from stress, increased heart problems and cortisol levels, and difficulties managing HIV/Aids.

REMEMBER THIS!!! Different factors may be responsible for the development of a disease at different points along its path. For example, a number of different things can contribute to the gradual deposition of fats in the arterial wall which underlies heart disease, and likewise the sudden rise in catecholamine production which leads to a coronary embolism. Both these physical processes can be triggered by the way an individual forms their 'judgement of threat' – the key stage in the assessment of risk which underpins the level of anxiety we experience and the way we deal with it.

Developing health problems

With the greater emphasis on preventative medicine and health education in recent times, the need to understand how disease develops and the factors which are involved is increasingly important. Many diseases have complex and lengthy developmental histories. Levels of emotional intelligence have been shown to influence susceptibility to health problems as well as their progression. There are a variety of risk factors (pertaining to your health) which are affected by the level of emotional intelligence you exercise:

Personality: Neuroticism is a personality trait that has been most often examined in relation to health behaviour. It is defined as the tendency to experience negative emotions including anger, anxiety and depression. It has been connected with poor health behaviour, principally the risks associated with drinking, smoking and drug abuse. It has also been suggested to be a risk factor for increasing stress levels with the associated risks of disease as a result. On the other hand, neurotic and anxious people may go to the doctor more often, resulting in possible earlier detection of health problems.

Ageing: In 2001, a longitudinal study of ageing and Alzheimer's disease looked at autobiographical sketches written by a group of several hundred older nuns on entering a convent some 40 to 60 years previously. The sketches were listed according to the number of positive statements they contained. The nuns in the lower half of the list died on average nine years sooner than those in the top half, with a significantly greater incidence of dementia. The difference in survival was not related to their lifestyle or circumstances in the intervening period but, it would seem, to their positive emotional intelligence six decades earlier. This finding is all the more remarkable because from their early twenties onwards, the lives of the nuns were as close to identical as human lives can be.

One frequently mentioned possibility is that as people age they become less involved with life around them and are therefore more passive and/or prone to ignore events, becoming more fatalistic about their ability to control them. There is evidence that older people are less emotionally responsive to environmental threats, including health threats, despite their levels of understanding. In some conditions (such as melanoma, cervical cancer and breast cancer) the lack of emotional responsiveness results in elderly people delaying for much longer before taking symptoms to their doctor and not taking up opportunities for diagnostic and preventative services.

Hostility and anger: Of all personality factors, the 'type A' cluster of behaviours (discussed further in the next section) has been the target of most study, and the findings associated with it have given more credence to the relevance of personality to health than any other factor. The construct was crystallized in the writing of two cardiologists, Friedman and Rosenman, who designated as 'type A' those individuals who characteristically display excessive achievement-striving, competitiveness, impatience, hostility, and vigorous speech and motor mannerisms.

The lower emotional intelligence displayed by type A people is characterized by a lack of self-awareness, inefficient emotional self-control and a tendency towards skewed thinking (see page 150) – all of which very often leads to low-quality relationships.

Follow-up studies on initially healthy men showed that those characterized as type A were more likely to develop heart disease than people in the general population. Following a great deal of scrutiny, however, the focus of interest is now more specifically on the effects of hostility, anger and anger expression. Hostility in particular appears to be a major contributory factor for heart disease, as well as higher lipid levels and body mass index. Hostility levels also have a direct relationship with behaviours like smoking and alcohol usage.

A, B, C and D type people

Three types of people, characterized by their prevalent emotional states, are at greater risk of 'adverse cardiovascular events' such as heart attacks, according to research in the Netherlands, UK and US. The 'at risk' groups that have been identified are:

- People who are driven, forceful and competitive

- Those whose behaviours are often hostile, angry and negative

- People who may be socially inhibited, anxious, stressed or depressed.

As described above, the first group are described as 'type A' people. The health risks for this type of person are not clear because several large studies have not found causal links with heart problems. They have, however, highlighted the way emotional intelligence (emotion, mood, self-control and relationship behaviours) might affect the heart. Characteristics of a 'type A' person's behaviour include impatience, intolerance of errors, pressure to hurry up, getting involved too much, excessive acquisition of possessions, failure to delegate and suspicion. They do not use emotional intelligence easily or well to collaborate with others nor can they relax with others when there is an opportunity to do so. As a result, they often experience stress.

People who are classified as having 'type B' personalities are better at relaxing without feeling guilty and working without becoming anxious or agitated. Some of their other characteristics include being more relaxed about time (they don't get overly stressed about being late), and not being easily angered.

Later work has identified how elements of emotional intelligence which are involved in type A behaviour can in fact help. There are some factors which might actually protect the heart (like the drive to succeed and the dedication to make healthy changes. You might like to try the questionnaire below, which assesses the balance you have between type A and type B behaviours. You need to be honest though!

The second 'at risk' group – those whose behaviours are often hostile, angry and negative – are sometimes characterized as 'type C' people. A category originally used in assessing the risks of poorly managed emotion pertaining to cancer, these individuals may be less driven but have a cognitive style involving negative automatic thinking, expressed in their reactions to others. They find it difficult to manage their emotions, frequently fluctuating between 'highs' and 'lows'. Overwhelmingly they exhibit hostility toward others and find it difficult to cope with them without becoming irritated and angry. They also find emotional intelligence difficult, both because of the difficulties they have controlling negative and aggressive instincts and because the levels of emotion they experience inhibits them in building positive relationships, with the mutual trust and tolerance needed.

'Type D' people have the same tendency to experience negative emotions as type C, but it becomes a driver for internally focused self-criticism, anxiety and depression. At the same time, they have difficulty building relationships due to social inhibition. Type D people are more closed in social interactions, are less likely to disclose their personal feelings toward others; they tend to feel a bit insecure. Emotionally intelligent doctors have described them as 'the type of patient that tells you everything is okay, that there are no problems. But you can sense that something is going on or something is not quite right.' This combination makes them more liable to chronic forms of psychological distress, leading to an absence of confidence.

The second of the questionnaires which follow will enable you to think about whether your behaviours qualify as 'type D' behaviour and what emotional intelligence you need for dealing with it.

Are you a stress-prone 'type A' personality?
Type A personalities tend to be more success-ful – and they also get 90 per cent of all heart attacks. Are you a type A? Here's a chance for you to test yourself. Below are two columns of contrasting behaviour. Since each of us belongs somewhere on a continuum between the two extremes, give yourself a score between 1 and 7 for each pair of statements, where 1 = the behaviour in the left-hand column and 7 = the behaviour in the right-hand column.

	Score (1–7)	
Doesn't mind leaving things temporarily unfinished		Must get things finished once started
Calm and unhurried about appointments		Never late for appointments
Not competitive		Highly competitive
Listens well; lets others finish speaking		Anticipates others in conversation (nods, interrupts, finishes sentences for others)
Never in a hurry, even when pressured		Always in a hurry
Able to wait calmly		Uneasy when waiting
Easygoing		Always going full speed ahead
Takes one thing at a time		Tries to do more than one thing at a time; thinks about what to do next
Slow and deliberate in speech		Vigorous and forceful in speech (uses a lot of gestures)
Concerned with satisfying self, not others		Wants recognition by others for a job well done
Slow doing things (e.g. eating, walking)		Fast doing things
Serene		Hard driving

	Score (1–7)	
Expresses feelings openly		Holds feelings in
Has a large number of interests		Few interests outside work
Satisfied with job		Ambitious – wants quick advancement at job
Never sets own deadlines		Often sets own deadlines
Feels limited responsibility		Always feels responsible
Never judges things in terms of numbers		Often judges performance in terms of numbers (how much, how many)
Casual about work		Takes work very seriously (works weekends, brings work home)
Not very precise		Very precise and careful about detail

Add up all your scores to give yourself a single overall score.

If you scored over 110 you are a type A1
If you are in this category, and especially if you are over 40 and smoke, you have a high risk of developing cardiac illness and other stress-related illnesses.

If you scored 80–109, you are a type A2

You are also a cardiac-prone personality but your risk of heart disease is not quite as high as a type A1.

Type A personalities generally have 'a stress problem' although most do not recognize this until extreme symptoms or serious illnesses develop. Type A behaviour is a learned personality pattern which is well rewarded in Western culture. It is a desired trait in most institutions, especially at a managerial level. In other parts of the world, however, these behaviours may take different, more culturally appropriate forms.

Development of the skills for emotional intelligence may be very important for type A personalities, to help develop effective relationships and to spot opportunities for growth or change. Type A people may need to work on the areas of self-awareness and emotional control first, to enable that to happen.

If your score is 60–79, you are a type AB

You are a mixture of type A and type B patterns. This is a healthier pattern than either A1 or A2, but you have the potential for slipping into type A behaviour and you should recognize this. The comments above regarding developing emotional intelligence also apply to you.

If your score is 59 or under, you are a type B

This personality complex is characterized by general relaxation and coping adequately with stress. You express few of the reactions associated with cardiac disease.

(This questionnaire is widely used in the UK's National Health Service and is based on a test developed by Dr Howard Glazer in 1978.)

'Type D' behaviour test

Below are a number of statements that people often use to describe themselves. For each, give yourself a score from 0–4, where 0 = false, 1 = rather false, 2 = neutral, 3 = rather true, 4 = true. There are no right or wrong answers: your own impression is the only thing that matters.

1. I make contact easily when I meet people.
2. I often make a fuss about unimportant things.
3. I often talk to strangers.
4. I often feel unhappy.
5. I am often irritated.
6. I often feel inhibited in social interactions.
7. I take a gloomy view of things.
8. I find it hard to start a conversation.
9. I am often in a bad mood.
10. I am a closed kind of person.
11. I would rather keep people at a distance.
12. I often find myself worrying about something.
13. I am often down in the dumps.
14. When socializing, I don't find the right things to talk about.
15. I think about myself often.

Scoring

The first step is to **reverse the scores** for questions **1** and **3**; that is, if you gave yourself 0, change it to 4; if you gave yourself 1, change it to 3; 2 stays as 2; 3 becomes 1; 4 becomes 0.

'Negative affectivity' scale: Add together your scores for questions 2, 4, 5, 7, 9, 12 and 13.

'Social inhibition' scale: Add together your scores for questions 1, 3, 6, 8, 10, 11 and 14.

You demonstrate type D behaviour if you scored 10 or higher on both negative affectivity and social inhibition scales. If you do, you might want to check out the sections of the book on skewed thinking (pages 150–153) and self-esteem (pages 52–56).

Psychological well-being

The overall quality of life and sense of fulfilment we enjoy is a major factor in our day-to-day mood. In the UK, the traditional connections between health and social care are now being expanded to include a broader definition of healthcare; this includes medical services, social work, healthy living initiatives, public health and care services. The label of choice is now 'health and well-being'.

Psychological well-being (PWB) is an idea closely related to emotional intelligence, suggesting that a number of factors are important for our overall happiness, healthy relationships and mental health. Research psychologist Carol Ryff's model of PWB reinforces the importance of EI in promoting a healthy and fulfilling lifestyle. It highlights the significance of:

- Self-acceptance – valuing yourself and what you think is important

- The establishment of quality ties to other individuals and groups

- A sense of autonomy in thought and action

- The ability to manage complex environments to suit personal needs and values

- The pursuit of meaningful goals and a sense of purpose in life

- Continued growth and development as a person.

Psychological well-being 'check-up'
The following statements all relate to aspects of psychological well-being. Consider whether you agree or disagree with each statement as it relates to you:

Autonomy: I have confidence in my opinions, even if they are contrary to the general consensus.

Environment: In general, I feel I am in charge of the situation in which I live.

Personal growth: I think it is important to have new experiences that challenge how you think about yourself and the world.

Positive relations with others: People would describe me as a giving person, willing to share my time, but not a pushover.

Purpose in life: Some people wander aimlessly through life, but I am not one of them.

Self-acceptance: I like most aspects of my personality.

The health effects of emotional intelligence

In 2003, several hundred volunteers took part in an EI and health trial, trying to establish whether emotional intelligence actually enhances the working of our immune systems. The trial involved training one group of volunteers in awareness of their own emotions and meditation. The other group were given no training. They were then given a flu injection to establish how strong an antibody response they would have to it. Six months after vaccination, the meditation group had produced almost twice as many antibodies as the control group. This evidence suggests strong support for the notion that positive emotional states, developed through working on emotional intelligence, can boost immune functions.

In a parallel study, they also found that the more optimistic the individual was (using both personality and practical tests), the lower the risk of developing a cold. Separate studies have shown that when people have less emotional control and become very excited, there is a greater risk of infection. More negative people just seemed to have an average risk.

Disease management

The role that emotional management plays in managing disease is a good illustration of how emotional intelligence can benefit patients, carers and health professionals.

If you know anyone who suffers with a chronic, debilitating condition, you will very likely be aware of the severe psychological effects that such illnesses can have. Sufferers often find it hard to adjust to a new way of being in the world, missing the things that made their life fun. They can feel like a burden on their family, leading to depression and/or anxiety. In such circumstances, emotionally intelligent health care staff can make a huge difference in helping patients manage their mental states, which, for some conditions, even affects the treatments clinicians may prescribe.

When people suffer from cancer, medical interventions range from procedures with a curative purpose (surgery to remove a tumour altogether) to palliative care in which the patient needs to learn how to live with cancer, accepting that it will not go away. The emotional aspects of cancer affect patients, their partners and families, and also the staff providing care. Most of those involved experience emotional distress. Some people develop severe anxiety, depression or other psychiatric syndromes. There is evidence that emotionality and a fighting spirit are beneficial for cancer patients' prognoses, while stoicism, fatigue and emotional inexpressiveness are harmful.

There is no doubt that emotional aspects of disease are central to patients' quality of life. Many of the common problems they experience can be minimized, provided that their importance is recognized. Desperation, fear, uncertainty, shock, denial, depression, self-doubt, frustration, fear of the future and loss of control are all features of living with chronic disease. Patients, carers and medical staff who understand emotional intelligence are better equipped to handle these problems. Medical staff who register body language or the way patients express themselves have a better and more immediate way of evaluating the information they are given; carers who learn to understand their own feelings of resentment can become more resilient; conversations with patients about care plans can be more effective when they are open and optimistic. And patients who understand their feelings and are mindful can stay positive and value their relationships.

Five ways to emotional intelligence through well-being

Those of us who try to nurture greater emotional intelligence in our lives sooner or later discover that it is most difficult to be self-aware, in control and aware of others just when it is most useful – when the pressure is on. When we feel bad or when there doesn't seem to be a moment to spare, mindfulness and being sensitive to emotions are major challenges. But these are the times when emotional intelligence can give us a solid foundation for the focus, decisiveness and positive frame of mind that is usually necessary.

Day to day, our own emotional well-being, and the emotional well-being of others who we value, are major health issues in their own right and can greatly affect physical health. Stress, depression and anxiety can contribute to a host of physical ailments including digestive disorders, sleep disturbances, cardiac problems and lack of energy. The effects on our immune system mean we are at risk of a wider range of physical ailments. The mind–body link is becoming increasingly recognized.

When life is particularly difficult and relationships are hard going, we can use important aspects of emotional intelligence. We need the capacity to name the feelings we are experiencing and understand what is causing them. We can use coping skills like relaxation, assertiveness, the drive to succeed, our sense of who we are and what's important to manage our feelings and remain positive. Maintaining a day-to-day position in which we value others, express our feelings and look out for them – helping wherever we can – is neither a luxury nor is it woolly-minded optimism. These are tools for managing the way emotion, mood, behaviour and social factors might affect our long-term health.

You might want to try the following five ways of boosting health and well-being through EI.

1. Connecting with others provides support, balance, enrichment, stability and a sense of community in your life. Make an effort to talk to wider groups of people than you would normally. Look at connecting with people as a foundation stone for your life and be prepared to invest time and energy into it. Listen to people you come across and watch their body language, registering the different signals and the 'music' behind the words. Think about your family, your work and your community. Connect with neighbours, colleagues, customers, friends and your family.

2. Be physically active, walking or running, playing a sport, doing some gardening, dancing, using a bike. Just go into the fresh air outside. Physical activity helps you feel good, giving you a sense of balance in your life. Exercise helps the autonomic nervous system rid your body of stress. Talk to your doctor about your mobility or fitness if you are concerned. But get outside and enjoy the fresh air.

3. Stay alert. Enjoy the choices others make about their clothing, style or appearance. Be curious. Register what is beautiful. Comment on the unusual. Notice how the trees change from season to season. Live in the moment, whether walking to the shops or driving to work, sharing food with friends or putting the world to rights over a drink. Savour the experience and be aware of how you feel just looking at others. Appreciate the look and feel, the smells and sounds of each moment; see even the ordinary experience of being in a crowd afresh by looking and listening closely both to you and to others.

4. Keep learning. Find opportunities to do something new in your work. Learn what others have valued, then try it yourself and think about how it feels. Rediscover an old interest. Enrol for evening classes in something you've never tried before. Learn to play music or sing. Set yourself an interesting and stimulating challenge. Use your skills in a different setting. Look at each bit of progress you make on something new as a success, enjoy it and let it boost your confidence.

5. Give. Try to empathize with someone who is doing something for nothing and work out what they are getting from it. Do a small, nice thing once a week, for someone you know or for a stranger. Look for people who may need help or support in some way in your local community or among your friends or family. Open a door for someone. Smile. Volunteer your time.

Think about getting some of your happiness from being part of a group, helping others. Watch someone receiving your help. Tell them they are helping you. Share their sense of being given something.

Conclusion

There is little doubt that many people have found the concept of emotional intelligence both interesting and useful in a wide variety of settings, from teaching to healthcare, from personal relationships and parenting to making work environments a more productive, positive and enjoyable place to be. I hope this book has helped you to appreciate how EI can improve your life, and shown you how you can develop your skills to achieve this.

This book has tried to describe a practical view of emotional intelligence (no doubt with less academic rigour than some would like). It has tried to balance the tools and knowledge you need for EI with as wide a range of perspectives and evidence as could be fitted in without submerging the reader.

Once or twice in the book we have touched on the great debate about the nature of EI: is it a mental ability or a mixture of personality traits, abilities and skills? I don't know. It is probably a blend of the two. I suspect that in the real world we take ideas from anywhere and use them to make our lives better – and there's a great deal of evidence that emotional intelligence can do that. But as with all talents and abilities, EI gets better with practice; the more mindful we are about what's happening around us, the richer life can be …

Further reading

A number of books about emotional intelligence have been published over the last few years. Some are very academic, precise and research-based; others are much more personal, often based on the experiences of the writer, and try to provide practical perspectives. Both have their value if you want to expand your knowledge of EI and get more information on the ideas contained in this book.

Here is a list of books which the author has found useful:

Emotions Revealed, Ekman (Weidenfeld & Nicolson, 2003)

Emotional Intelligence, Goleman (Bantam, 1995)

Emotional Intelligence: Key Readings on the Mayer and Salovey Model, Salovey, Brackett and Mayer (Dude Publishing, 2004)

Emotional Development and EI – Implications for Education, Salovey and Sluyter (Perseus Books, 1997)

The Mindful Way Through Depression, Williams, Teasdale, Segal and Kabat-Zin (Guilford Press, 2007)

Overcoming Anxiety, Stress and Panic, Williams (Hodder Arnold, 2010)

The Joy of Stress, Hanson (Pan, 1987)

Primal Leadership: Learning to Lead with Emotional Intelligence, Goleman, Boyatzis and McKee, (Harvard Business School Press, 2002)

Applied Emotional Intelligence: The Importance of Attitudes in Developing Emotional Intelligence, Sparrow and Knight (Wiley, 2006)

Emotional Intelligence: The New Rules, Yeung (Cyan Books, 2009)

Raising an Emotionally Intelligent Child, Gottman and DeClaire (Simon & Schuster, 1997)

The Language of Emotional Intelligence: The Five Essential Tools for Building Powerful and Effective Relationships, Segal (McGraw-Hill, 2008)

People Skills, Thompson (Palgrave MacMillan, 2009)

The Mind Gym: Relationships, Mind Gym (Sphere, 2009)

TA Today, Stewart and Joines (Lifespace Publishing, 1987)

Emotional Intelligence: Science and Myth, Matthews, Zeidner and Roberts (Cambridge, 2002)

Mindfulness for Beginners, Kabat-Zinn (Sounds True Inc., 2006)